Your Outta Control Bird

by Nikki Moustaki

T.F.H. Publications, Inc.
One TFH Plaza
Third and Union Avenues
Neptune City, NJ 07753

This book has been published with the intent to provide accurate and authoritative information in regard to the subject matter within. While every precaution has been taken in preparation of this book, the publisher and author assume no responsibility for errors or omissions. Neither is any liability assumed for damages resulting from the use of the information herein.

ISBN: 0-7938-2925-9

Printed and bound in USA

www.tfh.com

Contents

How Did
My Bird
Turn Into a
Monster?

Many people living with a pet bird often wonder why they wanted the darn thing in the first place. It screams. It bites. It pulls out its feathers. There's seed all over the floor. What kind of pet is this? Getting a pet bird seemed like a good idea at the time. The bird was so pretty, so quiet, so cuddly in the store. Or, the breeder swore the bird was well raised, sociable, and sweet. Aren't birds supposed to be easier to care for than dogs, less finicky than cats, hardly a bother at all?

Right. Many pet birds—the parrots in particular—are noisy, fussy, wild animals. They can be gentle, friendly,

Beware of Bird! Proceed with caution!

and loving, too, but that's on a good day. Living with a parrot is like living with a perpetual two-year-old child. But I don't have to tell you that. If you're reading this book, chances are you already know it firsthand.

Whether you live with a parakeet or a macaw, you live with a beast that has the potential, perhaps more than any other commonly kept animal, to become unruly and monstrous very quickly, and with little warning—that is, unless you take the time to understand your feathered friend, inside and out. If your bird is behaving like a feathered Attila the Hun, it's likely that there's something amiss in its life. This book will guide you though the basics of bird behavior, the nooks and crannies of bird-dom. Once you begin to understand your bird as an individual and take a close look at your relationship, you will discover the tools needed to deal with any behavior you consider a problem.

What Constitutes a "Monster" Bird?

Most people would define a "monster" bird as a bird that's not getting along in the household as it once did, one that's exhibiting exasperating behavior, one that isn't "itself" anymore. Birds should come with a warning tag: BEWARE! THIS PET MAY BECOME

How Did My Bird Turn Into a Monster?

UNRULY, LOUD, AND DANGEROUS. BUY WITH CAUTION. Unfortunately, birds don't come with a caution sticker, and many people discover the hard way that a bird isn't an easy animal to live with. Most people are unprepared for potential behavior issues, and they neglect the fact that a bird, like a child, grows through stages. Most birds won't be baby-cuddly forever.

A "monster" bird is a misunderstood, unhappy, or ill bird—bottom line. These three factors are the only reasons for a relationship between human and bird to deteriorate. There is a lot of conflicting information out there about bird behavior and bird care, but it's really a simple matter. Understanding your bird's physiology and psychology, interacting with your bird appropriately, and taking your bird to an avian

Birds aren't hatched as monsters – bad behavior is generally learned.

Problem Pollies

Most "monster" companion birds are in the psitticine family, better known as the parrots. These include the common parakeet (budgerigar or "budgie") and the giant hyacinth macaw. In the case of a "monster" bird, size doesn't matter. What matters is that the relationship between bird and guardian has deteriorated somehow, and whether the problem is a lovebird that has started to bite or a cockatoo that is plucking its feathers out, it has to be resolved to keep the relationship intact.

veterinarian regularly will go a long way toward preventing and solving problem behaviors. These things are simple, but they are also time-consuming. Properly taking care of a bird, both its physical and emotional needs, is a process that has to be repeated daily. A bird is not a "sometimes" playmate, but an everyday responsibility.

Perhaps your feathered pal is behaving like Godzilla, only worse, and if you wanted Godzilla, you would have bought a Gila monster instead. Perhaps the bird is trying to run the household, or has taken to cowering in fear and striking out when someone comes close. How about screaming, plucking, and biting? The most important thing to realize is that your bird is not doing these things "on purpose." Intention is not part of your bird's emotional life. Your bird is not sitting in its cage, plotting its next move. The bird is merely working on instinct with the tools that nature has given it. Unfortunately for the bird's human companions, a bird's instinctual tools are limited to life in the natural world. A bird's inner programming doesn't recognize life in a human home, and the conflict between its instincts and its environment is often the cause of "monster" behaviors. This is why it's so important for the bird's human friend to behave in a very specific manner, to house and feed the bird according to the bird's needs, and to adapt somewhat to the bird's life—not expect the bird to adapt perfectly to life with humans.

"Monster" behaviors can be as problematical for the bird as they are for its owners. In most cases, a bird doesn't prefer the "monster" behavior over "good" behavior. A bird will continue to repeat an unpleasant behavior, say, banging its beak repetitively on the cage bars, because that's the only way it has found to unleash some of its anxiety and energy. The behavior becomes a habit and continues simply because the behavior has become part of the bird's routine.

Sometimes a behavior that seems monstrous is actually completely natural, albeit strange or annoying to the humans involved in the bird's life. Figuring out the difference between a pathological behavior and a natural one is important to dealing with the problem. Many times the problem should be dealt with by acceptance rather than modification. Having the proper expectations and learning to accept a bird as an individual with special needs is important to forging a lasting bond.

Perhaps you've adopted, inherited, or have been given a "monster" bird. This is a bird with a problem that has habituated, a bird that is so entrenched in its behavior that the abnormal action seems normal.

This behavior will continue for the life of the bird unless measures are taken to change it for good. Birds, like humans, are creatures of habit, and those habits aren't easily broken. You didn't instill the "problem" behavior, which may make it easier to eliminate. Oftentimes, a simple, innocent behavior on the part of a human can inspire problem behavior, and a bird that has been introduced into a new household will be away from that prior stimulus, giving it a chance, perhaps, to change.

Parrots and Polar Bears

Part of what makes birds "monsters" is that they started out as monsters, and there's not much that a human companion can do about it. By "monster" I mean that birds are as wild as other animals we

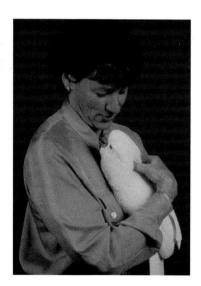

might consider monsters, like crocodiles or sharks. Would you ever expect to tame a crocodile or shark not to bite? Doubtful. It's impractical to have those kinds of expectations or to think that buying a crocodile or shark as a baby and treating it nicely will take the wildness out of it. The same holds true for parrots. A bird is much more than a list of its vital statistics, like its species, age, and sex; just like humans, birds are complicated creatures, products of both instinct and environment.

Regardless of the bond to humans, parrots are still wild animals.

Even though there is no "true" domesticated parrot, the budgie (parakeet) comes close.

Most people will agree that it would be inexcusable for the average pet owner—someone who lives in a modest apartment or house, works five days a week, and may have a family to care for—to own a polar bear. Even if that pet owner was a conscientious person, read all the books about the species, and loved the animal with an unrivaled passion, most people would agree that a home is not the proper place for a polar bear.

Parrots are just as wild as polar bears. There is no such thing as a domesticated parrot, one whose internal traits have been changed to suit the needs of humans. Like the polar bear, the bird's wild spirit remains intact. Even birds that have been bred in captivity, have never met another bird, and were fed only a manufactured diet (like pellets), behave just like their wild counterparts until they are presented with situations where they have to adapt, such as interacting with humans in a home, rather than other birds in a rainforest.

A hand-reared bird would fly away if given the opportunity, and it would probably be able to live the rest of its life without human assistance if the environment was right. This has been proven in temperate places such as southern Florida, where there are many flocks of different types of birds living as well as they would in their countries of origin. Some birds that fly away do find their owners again or search out another human, but I suggest that these birds are in the minority. These birds were probably treated well enough by their human guardians that they wanted to return to "the good life," where food, water, and safety were abundant.

A bird choosing to be in the company of humans is the first signal of domestication, but the parrot family on the whole has a long way to go before it's considered truly domestic. The exceptions to this rule are the parakeet and the cockatiel, two parrots that have been bred in captivity far longer than any others. These birds are close to being domesticated, but because they are generally bred for visual traits and not personality or behavioral traits, they are not much closer to true domestication than any other. Even the meanest cockatiels are allowed to breed if they're pretty and will produce pretty offspring. That is standard practice in the bird community today, though this is slowly changing.

Why Aren't Birds Bred for Behavioral Traits?

The bird stock in the United States is limited to the birds that were already here before the Convention in International Trade in Endangered Species act (CITES) in the 1990s made importing wild-caught birds illegal. This means that breeders have to work inside a closed system, and rather than have a vicious macaw taking up space, it will be bred, regardless of the behavioral traits it may pass along to its offspring.

Birds are judged primarily by what's on the outside, but most are more than just a "pretty face."

Also, birds are judged more for their exterior appearance than how they behave. Parrots are aesthetically pleasing to humans, and breeders capitalize on this by breeding flashy birds together to produce babies that are equally flashy and, therefore, more salable.

Have you ever been to a bird show where parrots are being exhibited against one another? Birds at bird shows are judged on their looks alone. At a dog or cat show, the animal must be docile and polite. Not so with birds. A bird just needs to sit pretty on the perch and show off its perfect composition. Unlike dog competitions, there are no agility, obedience, or other

Here to Serve?

Think of the other domesticated animals we commonly live with: cats can be mousers, horses can be transportation, and cows can be beasts of burden. Sometimes a domesticated animal seems to serve no purpose, such as the toy dog, but they were bred just to be pets and lapdogs. There's no such thing as a lap-bird, or, as it commonly misrepresented, a cage-bird. Thinking of a bird as cage-bird is silly. That's like thinking of an oak tree as a houseplant—sure, you can keep an oak tree in a pot, but at some point it needs to be replanted or it will outgrow the pot and die. Lawn grass is domesticated; oak trees are not.

ability trials for birds. Birds are judged by their covers, so to speak, which is part of the reason why they haven't been domesticated—but that's not the whole story.

Domestication requires that a species be changed over time to suit the needs of human beings. Domestication also serves the species in that it no longer has to fend for itself, but it allows certain liberties to be removed from its life in order for it to have an abundance of the things it needs, such as food, water, and shelter. Some animals, like the dog, have natural programming that lends itself toward domestication. This isn't a conscious act on the part of the species, but a natural genetic encoding allowing domestication to happen over time.

How Did My Bird Turn Into a Monster?

Dogs have been bred for thousands of years to serve humans in various tasks—herding, vermin hunting, retrieving, guarding, and so on. Humans needed a dog to perform a task, say, having a pesky badger dug out of a hole. The properly shaped dog for that had to be skinny and low to the ground. Dogs having these desired traits were bred together, and the traits were refined over time though line breeding, until a dog emerged that was skinny and low enough to help clear vermin off of a farmer's land—the Dachshund.

What could a parrot possibly do to help humans live easier, better lives? What could a polar bear do? Part of what we love about these animals is that they're wild. Having a parrot is like bringing a little piece of the rainforest (or savanna, plain, or mountain range) into your home. The only possible factor that anyone could possibly want to change about the bird, on the whole, is to make it more docile. But could you imagine a docile polar bear? Would it be able to get along in the wild? Not a chance. The same holds true for the parrot. Perhaps someday, when aviculturists succeed in "trait breeding" parrots for personality and behavior and not for exterior beauty, the result might be an animal resembling a domesticated parrot, but I am willing to assert that there will be "throwbacks" in every generation, individual birds that resemble their wild cousins in spirit as well as appearance. Even dogs, as domesticated as they are, still turn around and around before they plop down to sleep, making a nice nest in the imaginary tall grass that their instincts tell them is still there.

Be a Bird

Try, for a moment, to put yourself into your bird's place. Sit down and close your eyes and really try to imagine that you are your bird. What is your housing like? Do you like what you eat? Do you get fresh food each day, including vegetables and fruit? Is your water clean? How often do you get to see and interact with your favorite person? Do you have enough to do all day? When was the last time you visited the doctor? If the answers to any of these questions sent up a red flag for you, then it might be time to learn more about what your bird needs and how to provide it.

Essential "Birdness"

To understand why your bird has changed for the worse or is having a specific problem, you should know what constitutes normal behavior and what doesn't. There are so many books written about human psychology—the self-help section in the bookstore is loaded with texts on understanding how people behave and how to interpret the behavior—but there's a kind of unawareness, whether it's purposeful or not, of the fact that animals have complexities and shades of feelings and moods just like we do. Many of their likes and dislikes, needs and desires, are preprogrammed, just as are many of ours, and to recognize the root of a bird's problem and then solve it, you must reach a basic understanding of what it means to be a bird.

Many people come to me for "problems" that their bird is having that turn out to be completely normal behaviors but are just being misinterpreted by their owners. Birds can be unusual and strange to the initiated, and not all of their normal behaviors are pleasant to their human friends.

Turn Annoyance Into Acceptance

Normal avian behaviors that annoy the humans in a bird's life are only a problem for those who do not have the tolerance to deal with a bird's quirks and personality shifts and who should possibly have another type of pet. Lack of understanding and tolerance are the primary reasons why birds end up neglected, abused, and re-homed. Coming to understand what the normal behaviors are and when they occur can help turn annoyance into acceptance. Here are some of the most commonly misinterpreted rules of avian behavior:

* Birds are preprogrammed to behave like wild animals and nothing will change that fact.

The problem that most birds face is that they are not allowed to live as they are meant to live. A parrot is put into a cage, given a minimum of attention, improper nutrition, and inadequate ways of expressing its "birdness," and is then expected to behave as a sweet, loving pet. Birds want to fly, chew, bond (with another bird or a human), nest, and get enough sleep. Seems simple, doesn't it? But for most birds living in a home environment, these simple needs aren't met. That's because birds don't want these things just

Trying to meet your bird's needs goes a long way toward preventing "monster" behaviors.

Seeing eye to eye isn't always easy, but it's worth trying.

some of the time. A bird requires its needs met 24 hours a day, 7 days a week, for the duration of its life. This is a grand order for a bird's human companion, who is, by nature, limited when it comes to having a relationship with another species, especially an essentially wild one. No matter how much time you spend with your bird, it will want more, unless its life mimics the life it would have in the wild to a degree that it doesn't feel confined and put-upon.

Birds are programmed to live by patterns. The rising and setting of the sun and the seasons engender different behaviors in a bird, an animal that is extremely sensitive to changes in light and temperature. Think of your bird as a computer. Behaviors are stored on the hard drive, all of the programs needed to make the individual unit function. There's no way to delete any of the programs, and if you try, the computer will crash. Big problems!

* Birds are control freaks, not unlike many other animals, including humans.

Birds are creatures of routine and will not do well with a family whose life changes drastically at regular intervals. Birds often begin problem behaviors after a significant change, like a move, new furniture, the addition of a baby or another pet to the family, or even a change in its owner's appearance. Birds like repetitiveness and do not tire of a strict routine as long as the routine is fulfilling and caters to the bird's needs. There should be some variation inside of the routine, such as new toys or new sounds to listen to, but the routine itself should remain intact.

* When left to its own devices, a bird will find a way to solve its problems and anxiety by itself, and the bird's solutions aren't always the best ones.

Here's a simple analogy: A child sucks a thumb because the behavior is soothing and reassuring. The parents have perhaps taken away the child's pacifier or won't let the child sleep in their bed anymore, and this can be distressing to the child, who looks for comfort, and may find it by sucking a thumb. The child has found a way to assert himself, to take care of the problem alone. The parents might not like this new behavior because it might eventually alter the child's teeth, so the parents will try to stop it, which

Stimulating Solution

Several years ago, the Central Park Zoo had a problem with one of their polar bears, Gus, a 700-pound male that started exhibiting neurotic, repetitive behavior and wouldn't consort with the two females in his habitat. They brought in an animal behaviorist, who discovered that Gus was suffering from the lack of stimulation of the type he would have had in the wild. It wasn't enough that he had a large habitat that mimicked his natural environment or that he had friends to play with. Zookeepers developed games for him, hiding food and so on, and Gus snapped out of his neurotic patterns and began behaving like his typical polar bear self again.

is difficult, but not impossible. Changing the unwanted action takes a program of behavior modification, which, if done through substitution and reward, is effective and preserves the child's emotional health.

A physically healthy bird that starts plucking its feathers out is like a child sucking its thumb. Something is missing in the bird's life, whether it's security or attention, and the bird is trying to reclaim control of its needs, even if that means acquiring a behavior that can be destructive. Often, the only measure a bird has to comfort or assert itself is a behavior that drives its human companion nuts and can be self-destructive to the point of creating a serious health issue. A bird that is beak banging, cage dancing, plucking, or repeating any other neurotic behavior that serves no practical purpose is a bird that is unhappy and is trying to find a means to take its mind off of the situation.

✳ Birds don't like to be alone.

In the wild, a parrot rarely spends much time alone. It goes from its parents' nest to the community at large and then finds a mate and has chicks of its own. It's a busy, social creature, with complex communication skills adapted over many thousands of years to living among others of its kind. This is not to say that a bird with only a human pal can't be happy, but the human pal must compensate for the lack of a natural social structure by providing the bird with abundant attention. Many birds can learn to play on their own for a time, but toys do not substitute for a living friend. Replicating the interactions a bird would have in the wild among its own kind is a tall order, almost impossible, but the person who has a lot of time to offer an avian friend, or who provides a natural environment for multiple birds, is one step ahead of most.

✳ Birds are purposeful.

Birds behave in certain ways for a good reason. Only neurotic or poorly socialized birds repeat behaviors that serve no purpose

Anxiety can cause birds to puck. Note this umbrella cockatoo's naked chest.

for their well-being. The bird's primary purpose is to stay alive and have its needs met, which is basically every organism's primary purpose. Normal behaviors, such as screaming at certain times during the day, chewing objects, and flying, serve the bird well. These behaviors have to do with finding safety, breeding, acquiring food, and so on, behaviors that help to keep the bird alive.

Problem behaviors, such as plucking and excessive screaming, also serve the bird well, but only because its basic needs aren't being met in the first place, and it has had to abandon its normal behavior for an abhorrent one in hopes that the new way of behaving will help to meet its needs. Often, the new behavior is disturbing to the bird's guardian, who might then help to make the behavior worse by unintentionally reinforcing it.

Monster Birds Are Often Bored

Birds in the wild have a lot to do all day, including finding food, finding water, attracting a mate, preening and grooming, playing, nesting, rearing young—all the while making sure they are safe from predators. Sure, they have time to nap, and after all that hard work, why not?

It's not difficult to see how different the companion bird's daily life is. Much of the companion bird's time is spent sitting in a cage, waiting to be let out, and no amount of wooden chew toys are going to make up for what the bird is missing—a full and natural life.

Forever Wild

Your bird is essentially a wild animal with the intense drive to socialize, so it will not be happy stuck in a cage all day, alone, even if the cage is huge and filled with toys. A bird has the emotional capability of a two-year-old child. Does your bird's behavior make more sense now that you know that? Imagine putting a very bright two-year-old child into a room by himself with a bunch of toys and some cereal and water. How long before he begins to cry? How long before he begins to cry and stomp his feet? How long before he's crying, stomping his feet, tossing the cereal against the walls, and throwing himself on the floor? Enough said.

A bird that is not getting its needs met, that has nothing to do all day but chew on a couple of wooden toys and climb up and down its cage bars, is bound to develop some "monster" behaviors. It's only natural for a bored, unhappy animal to find some way to occupy itself, and more often than not, that occupation turns into neurotic, repetitive behavior. This can include excessive screaming, cage dancing, plucking, and other disturbing behaviors that worry the humans in a bird's life, and for good reason. A bird that's exhibiting these behaviors is stressed out, and stress can lead to a decrease in the effectiveness of the immune system, which can lead to illness, and even death.

Punishment and Reward

It is impossible to punish a bird. Let me repeat: It is

Accentuate the Positive

Positive reinforcement instills behavior in animals (and people), and punishment removes behavior. It's far easier, with any animal, to instill a behavior than to remove one, especially one that has become a habit. If the bird receives no stimulus from a behavior that you would like to change, but receives tremendous stimulus from a behavior that you would like the bird to continue, you should wind up with a bird you can live with. The trick is to be consistent and to make sure everyone else that interacts with the bird is consistent, too. Changing behavior takes time and will not happen overnight; though I have seen new "problem" behaviors begin to change in a day or two.

impossible to punish a bird. Birds don't understand reprimand the way we do, and they may either find the punishment exciting, or, if the punishment is severe, terrifying. Birds don't learn well when they're frightened. Hitting a bird will never work to eliminate a "problem" behavior. The same goes for throwing shoes at it, dunking it in water, or any other type of physical abuse. This type of behavior is considered animal cruelty, and it is reprehensible and criminal.

Birds learn very well using a system of reward and positive reinforcement. The tricky thing about it is that if you don't know what stimulus to use and when to use it, you can easily reinforce a negative behavior and eliminate a positive one. For example, a bird that has never bitten before presses down a little bit too hard on your finger and you react with a loud "Ouch!" and jump up, yell at the bird, and put it back in its cage. While you're opening your medicine cabinet and getting your bandage, your bird is feeling great, thinking, "Wow, what a rush! I'm going to do that again!" Birds love big reactions and will continue to repeat a behavior as long as they get it. If there's no reaction, the behavior becomes boring and is replaced by another behavior, one that might get the reaction the bird wants.

A little nibble is no cause for alarm – just don't reinforce the behavior with an inappropriately large reaction.

The bird that has just learned to bite will try it again. If you don't react when you get another little nip, but do react with high praise when your bird snuggles you or steps on to your finger without biting, you are reinforcing these desirable behaviors. This is not to say that a bird that doesn't get a reaction from biting will never bite again (there are many reasons for biting), but it will ensure that you're not training it to bite by positively reinforcing the behavior.

Birds are drama addicts. If birds were people, they'd be into gambling, prize fighting, and sky diving. But, as birds, their drama consists of seeing if they can get a reaction from the humans and other animals around them. They'll tease a cat or dog and squawk and bite until their guardians get fed up and cause a scene— but only if these behaviors work to cause the exciting scene. If not, then the bird will cease using the problem behavior (biting, screaming, etc.) and will try something else. It's important to recognize what the new behavior is and reward it with high praise. If you fail to recognize the new behavior and praise it, the bird may try something else you don't like.

Making a Monster

Programming a bird to become a "monster" is simple, and most novice owners do a great job of it. Give the bird a lot of mixed messages, and when the bird is good and crazy, change everything around and mix up the messages some more. Let's look at a typical example: Say that a previously quiet bird (read: a bird emitting normal vocalizations) is beginning to scream in a way that it hadn't before. The screaming is about to get the bird's guardians kicked out of their apartment, not to mention that the noise is driving them nuts.

Screaming at a screaming bird only makes it scream louder.

The bird's guardians trained their dog to stop nuisance-barking, so they decide that they can train their bird to stop "nuisance screaming." Every time the bird screams, they yell back with a loud "No!" and it begins to scream louder and with more frequency—what a fun game! Screaming back doesn't work, so every time the bird screams they give it a nut. This works for the time the bird is eating the nut, but then it starts screaming again—in fact, it now screams every time it wants a nut, so it's screaming more. They fill a spray bottle with water and squirt it at the bird each time it screams. This terrifies the bird and it screams louder and cowers—or the bird is happy to have a bath. They rattle a can full of pennies when the bird is being noisy, and the bird stops for a moment, distracted momentarily by the sound, then screams even more. They try covering the cage when the bird screams, and this works for a few minutes, but not for the long term—the bird screams from beneath the cover. They can't stand the noise anymore, and the neighbors are even angrier, so they put the bird's cage into a dark closet and then make some phone calls to find it another home.

What happened? Why didn't their efforts work? Instead of punishing the bird, they were rewarding and/or scaring it. A nicely placed squirt of water might deter a dog from barking at the mail carrier, but it won't permanently silence a bird. The problem here is that the owners never took the time to find out the cause of the screaming. A bird that's displaying dis-turbing or neurotic behavior needs a detective, not an impatient guardian. Quick fixes work in the short term, but they do not solve the problem for good. Some of the actions they took could have been use-ful if they followed up with another, more useful action, but they hadn't taken the time to find out about birds and how they learn, and the end result was typical. The bird found a new home. How long will the bird stay there?

Food reward doesn't really work for birds unless they are very hungry, and I don't recommend starving a bird for training purposes. However, you might find that there's a particular food that your bird loves and will do anything for. Millet spray and certain types of nuts or fruit may work. Fun objects, such as toilet paper rolls, knots of fabric, and other things your bird craves (mine prefer pen caps) make good rewards. Show your bird that being "good" is fun.

Too Many, Too Little, Too Late

Bird people are more likely than any other pet owner to become overwhelmed, overcome, and overloaded with their companion of choice. Most people understand a certain number of dogs, cats, or fish are all they can have and still be able to maintain order, health, and compatibility. Even a pond owner knows not to overstock the pond with fish, or risk the delicate biological balance going awry and killing the whole lot.

Not so with bird lovers. We buy, order, adopt, and collect birds with abandon. Why not? They live in cages, they are easy to maintain, and they are loveable and beautiful; this one needs a home, that one needs a mate, and so on, until there are more cages in the house than furniture. It's very difficult for someone to give even one bird the kind of attention and social life it needs and desires, much less a whole flock. But it's so easy to become overloaded with birds.

Birds require a lot of hands-on attention to be happy and well-adjusted. That's how they live in the wild, with a mate and lots of other birds around. Most birds don't live alone if they can help it. Getting a friend for a lonely bird does not mean that the two birds will get along, it just means that now you have two birds that need love, care, and attention.

Part of preventing "problem" bird behavior is not overloading yourself with too many birds!

One parrot per family makes a good companion.

My suggestion to bird owners is to quit while they're ahead—or behind—whatever may be the case, and stick with the birds they have already, even if the bird is disappointing them at the moment. Some people keep acquiring birds because they feel sorry for them at the pet shop, their current birds aren't what they thought they were going to be, and so on, and then end up with more than they can handle. This leads easily to "monster" bird behavior because none of the birds are getting all of their needs met.

Outside
Influences
on Behavior
Problems

In This Chapter You'll Learn:

* The Human/Bird Bond
* How to find an avian veterinarian
* Understanding what makes birds sick
* How feeding, housing and grooming birds makes a difference

S ometimes a "problem parrot" results not from anything a parrot's guardian is actively doing, but from one or more of a parrot's basic needs not being met. This is a very common situation and is often easily remedied by learning what your parrot needs and then providing those needs exactly. This may mean revising how you view and interact with your parrot and how you maintain your parrot's health and well-being.

Parrots do not thrive on a bare minimum of anything. They need a bounty of attention, freedom and space, nutritious foods, and regular medical checkups.

Anything less will result in a "monster" bird that is far less pleasurable than the friend you had intended to enjoy when you brought the bird home.

How Do You Perceive Your Parrot?

Is your parrot a pet, a friend, or something to match with the drapes? (The latter is just a joke, I hope!) The word "pet" implies a relationship based on a social hierarchy where one part of the duo is dominant over the other. One individual is the pet and one individual is the owner, and those positions are not interchangeable.

"Friendship" implies a relationship based on equality, trust, dignity, and love. Rather than "pet and owner," I prefer the terms "friend and guardian," interchangeable positions that embody the qualities listed above. You are your parrot's friend, but you also are responsible for making sure it is properly cared for. This is a tricky relationship, because it's easy to forget that just because you're taking care of all of your parrot's needs, you aren't superior to it as an individual or above it in the social structure that makes up your relationship.

How is your parrot your guardian? A healthy bond between a parrot and a human can be intense and indestructible, and a parrot will do whatever it can to keep its human from harm, including shooing away interlopers (the guardian's spouse or human friends, in some cases) and warning the human of trouble, such as a hawk flying overhead (perception is everything, isn't it?), burglars, and fire. The parrot is a vigilant individual, and it's looking after you, whether you know it or not.

Even though a parrot is a member of a certain species, whether it's a cockatoo, lovebird, or caique, each individual is unique, just as each human is unique. Even though we share some of the same qualities with our fellow human beings, there are also qualities about us that make us different from others. Reading a book on a particular parrot species is a great way to get to know the species, but getting to know an individual parrot takes patience, a keen eye, and the willingness to see a bird as more than just a pretty face.

The parrot/human bond can be intense and indestructible.

Part of how people view parrots comes from how they are commonly seen in the public sphere. There are commercials on television showing parrots housed in inadequate cages or standing on bare perches, talking cleverly into the phone, and so on. Print ads aren't much better, and movies are perhaps the worst offenders, portraying parrots as witty, charming friends or as decoration in small cages in the background of a camera shot. These impressions of parrots are dangerous, implying that a bird is only

Studies on African grey parrots have proven that they are sentient and have vast cognitive abilities.

a pet, a thing whose natural habitat is nothing more than a cage and a perch, and whose only job in life is to amuse the humans around it.

Bird Brains

Dr. Irene Pepperberg of the Alex Foundation has been conducting research on the cognitive skills of African grey parrots since 1977. Her oldest colleague, Alex, is an African grey parrot that she purchased from a pet store. Over the years Alex has proven to have the cognitive abilities equivalent to those of a four-year-old child. He can positively identify colors, shapes, and distinct objects. He can count, and he understands complicated concepts such as here and away. He is sentient (having a sense of self) and he even teaches himself things he wants to know, such as new colors or names of objects. He asks clearly to take a shower, be put back into his cage, and for specific foods that he likes. Alex has shown that primates aren't the only animals that are capable of this type of learning, complicated problem solving, and set-making.

No wonder so many parrots become unhappy in captivity. They aren't challenged, and it's easy for an unchallenged, extremely intelligent being to become unhappy and neurotic. And it's not just the grey parrot that has the capacity for this kind of brainpower. People who live with macaws, conures, quakers, and other types of parrots report that their birds utter words and phrases in context. It's important to remember how capable and smart a parrot is and to respect and cater to its intelligence, not overlook it. A bird with too little to do is a good candidate for behavioral issues.

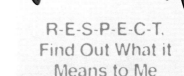

R-E-S-P-E-C-T. Find Out What it Means to Me

The first step to solving a parrot's behavior issue is to really internalize the fact that your parrot is an individual with unyielding wants, needs, and desires, and that its role in life is not to serve or amuse you, but to be a parrot, plain and simple. A parrot is intelligent, sensitive, and adaptable, and when these qualities are respected and the bird is treated with dignity, it will meet its capacity as an easy-to-live-with, loveable friend.

Is Your Monster Bird Feeling Well?

Very often a behavior problem coincides with a health problem. A parrot can have a low-grade health issue or unattended injury for quite a while, and it

Finding a Veterinarian

The Association of Avian Veterinarians can help
you locate an avian vet near you.
The Association of Avian Veterinarians
P.O. Box 811720
Boca Raton, FL US 33481-1720
Phone: 561-393-8901
Fax: 561-393-8902
http://www.aav.org

can become cranky, tired, loud, and self-mutilating. In many cases, the bird continues to suffer while its guardian is looking for an environmental or behavioral cause.

An avian veterinarian is your first stop when you notice a problem behavior starting. An avian veterinarian is a doctor who specializes in treating the diseases and injuries of birds. This doctor has studied the anatomy and physiology of birds and sees many bird clients each day. A veterinarian that treats dogs and cats and small animals may not know enough about birds to truly diagnose a health issue, even if he or she claims to be able to treat birds. Birds have very different physiological traits than mammals, and it takes a trained specialist to properly identify avian illnesses.

Once you've found an avian veterinarian near you, visit the office before taking your bird there. You should know the best route to get there quickly and choose the office closest to you. Birds are fragile creatures and can rapidly succumb to an injury, and you don't want to waste valuable time driving to an office that's far from your home.

Visit the office before you take your bird there and ask a few questions designed to evaluate whether or not you want that particular veterinarian working on your birds. You have a right to take your bird to the most qualified doctor, and you don't have to settle for a veterinary office that's not up to par with your expectations. Here are some important questions to ask:

Poison Control

The sudden onset of a severe behavioral problem might be an indication of an illness or injury, or even of poisoning. If you suspect poison, rush your bird to the doctor; if you can't reach the doctor immediately, call the Animal Poison Control Center at 888-4ANI-HELP (888-426-4435).

❋ How long have you been treating birds exclusively?
❋ Do you have birds of your own?
❋ What's your emergency policy? Will you come in on a day off if there's a serious problem?
❋ Do you treat many (your species of bird)?
❋ How do you deal with behavioral issues?

Look around the office. Is it clean? Is the staff friendly and helpful? Are there other people in the waiting room with their own birds awaiting treatment? Does the veterinarian's business card list avian veterinary medicine as his or her specialty? Some parrots can live to be 80 years old, so you'll want to develop a good relationship with your avian doctor.

Screaming, plucking, biting, and other undesirable behaviors can be linked to an illness, an injury, or a surge in hormones. Your avian veterinarian will run a battery of tests to try to find out why your bird is behaving oddly. There will be blood tests and swabs for cultures, as well as a physical examination.

Illnesses That Can Affect Behavior

I'm not a veterinarian, and I do not recommend using a book to definitively identify an illness or injury in your bird, but I can give you a few tips about what to look for so that you can report it to your avian veterinarian, which may help the doctor to make a diagnosis. The following are illnesses and injuries to rule out before you begin working with your bird's behavioral issues. Your bird might not be a "monster" after all, but might just be too ill to be its cheerful self.

Feather plucking may be a result of an illness, injury, or nutritional disorder.

Respiratory Problems: A bird that's having respiratory problems may pluck around the area of discomfort, the chest and belly area in particular. A bird's respiratory system is very delicate, and even a bird that has recovered from a respiratory ailment might still pluck the area that once bothered it. Symptoms of respiratory distress include panting, tail bobbing (the tail moving back and forth when the bird is sitting still), mucous or other bubbly discharge coming from the nose or mouth, and unconsciousness. Have your avian doctor check for aspergillosis, goiter, and vitamin deficiency.

A bird that's not feeling well might not want to be touched.

Skin and Feather Disorders: There are many skin and feather disorders that can cause a bird to pluck or self-mutilate. Birds with thyroid problems or internal bacterial infections may also pluck. Skin and feather ailments are generally easy to spot because they cause visual symptoms that include crusty beak and/or legs, overgrown beak, tumors, feather loss in patches, and abnormal feather growth. Have your avian doctor check for scaly face mites, Psitticine Beak and Feather Disease, liver disease, skin infections, as well as papillomas and other kinds of tumors. Plucking can also result from dietary deficiencies.

Foot Disorders: A parrot that once stepped easily on to your hand and now refuses to lift a toe for you might have a foot problem or injury. Gout, bumblefoot, mites, paralysis, and leg and foot injury are among the many possible causes.

Digestive Problems: Behavior associated with digestive disorders includes listlessness, regurgitation, inability to eat, and fluffed feathers. Symptoms include undigested seed in the droppings, strangely colored droppings (red, black, dark brown, etc.), and diarrhea. Have your avian veterinarian check for psittacosis, roundworms, proventricular dilation syndrome, candida infection, giardia, and polyoma virus.

Reproductive Problems: A female bird that is panting, crouching on the bottom of her cage, and behaving cranky may be trying to pass an egg that has gotten stuck in her oviduct. Symptoms include an extended, swollen abdomen, discharge from the vent, and partial or total paralysis of the legs. Place her in a hospital cage (you can use a fish tank with a heating pad underneath half of it and paper towels in the bottom), cover it partially, and place it in the bathroom. Run a hot shower so that the room becomes steamy (don't wet the bird). Heat and humidity, as well as a few drops of mineral or olive oil placed in her mouth and in her vent usually helps the egg pass. If it doesn't pass in a couple of hours, take her to the avian veterinarian, who may have to perform surgery to remove the egg.

Injury: An injury will make a bird cantankerous pretty quickly, although I've seen birds with tremendous, even fatal injuries that stay sweet and loving until the last breath. An injury that isn't obvious, such as an injury to the hips or breast-bone may elude an owner who might think that the bird doesn't want attention anymore because it won't step up like it used to. Injuries, even small ones, can initiate plucking and self-mutilating behavior, both of which must be addressed by an avian veterinarian before being addressed by a behaviorist.

Hormones and Maturity

Parrots experience the stages of infancy, early childhood, adolescence, and adulthood just as humans do. Though they look the same on the outside during each stage, there are significant changes going on inside. The smaller parrots, such as the parakeet, cockatiel, lovebird, and parrotlet, come into maturity fairly quickly, at eight months to one year of age. The medium-size birds, such as the conures, caiques, the birds in the poicephalus family, and the quakers can reach full maturity at two to four years of age. The larger birds, such as the African grey, Amazon, macaw, and cockatoo will start maturing sexually at five to eight years of age. It is often around this time that certain birds will become unruly, and even dangerous.

During a parrot's infancy and childhood, before the adolescent hormones kick in, most parrot guardians are tickled with their bird's affectionate behavior and funny antics. Once those hormones start surging, however, it can be another story. Some birds become very territorial, aggressive, and loud when mating season rolls around. Other behaviors may arise out of frustration, such as plucking and serious hostility. The parrot's guardians are naturally

Medication

Never use medications intended for human use without being directed to do so by your avian veterinarian. Some of the medicines we use can be toxic to birds, and there is not proper dosage information on the package for parakeets!

confused by this behavior. Where did the sweet baby go? How could the bird change so drastically?

Many people can't handle a bird that's going through a hormonal phase and they will give it away or set it up for breeding. These are unfortunate circumstances, because a little understanding and a few changes in environment can alter hormonal behavior significantly. Hormonal changes are a natural part of a parrot's development, and it shouldn't be punished for growing up.

Amazon parrots and cockatoos are notorious for hostile and unpredictable hormonal behavior. Both of these birds have a powerful beak and are fearless to a fault. Both Amazons and cockatoos are loud birds that get louder when they're in a hormonal period, and cockatoos are known to pluck and chew their feathers as well. These two species are given away, abandoned, or neglected more than any other for these reasons. In truth, the little lovebird is just as territorial and aggressive during mating season, but its size and small beak make it easier to deal with than the large Amazon or cockatoo.

Just as human/parent behavior must change when a child becomes a teenager, a bird's guardian must change his or her behavior to deal properly with a sexually mature bird. Both teenagers and sexually mature parrots are likely to run rampant if clear boundaries aren't created and kept. Consistency is the key, as are realistic goals and expectations.

Amazon parrots are notorious for seasonal hormonal behavioral problems.

Hormonal Behaviors

Most birds are programmed to breed at the time of year when the period of daylight gets longer and the period of darkness gets shorter (the exceptions are birds that have a natural habitat close to the equator). In most places, this happens in the springtime, when the photo period is extended and the evenings get brighter. Look for alterations in your sexually mature parrot's behavior around the time that you set your clocks ahead. Here are a few behaviors you might notice come springtime:

Regurgitation

Parrots use regurgitation to feed one another and their chicks. Regurgitation is a sign of a bond between two birds, and a parrot doesn't realize that its special human companion, who the bird has bonded to in lieu of another bird, might not appreciate it. In general, it is the male of the species that exhibits this courting and mating behavior. A regurgitating parrot will bob its head up and down a few times and then offer the mouthful of predigested food to its beloved. I have a male Meyer's parrot that does this every time I walk by his playpen. He likes to "feed" the space between my index and middle finger, though just in gesture—no food actually comes out of his beak. I've heard of parrots that like to "feed" their human's ears or nostrils. Humoring the bird will reinforce the bond between you, but don't let the behavior get excessive, or the bird might switch into full-blown breeding mode and exhibit less desirable behaviors. A parrot that's regurgitating by itself (to nobody, not even to a toy), with the vomit crusting around its beak and on its chest, may be ill and needs to see an avian veterinarian right away.

A Cockatoo in full display will fluff his feathers, raise his crest, and strut around like the king of the roost.

Displaying

A male parrot in full-blown breeding mode will "display," that is, strut around like the king of the roost, flapping his wings and swaying his head, flaring his tail feathers, and become an attention-hog in general. This is the courtship dance that the male parrot would use in the wild to attract a female. If the bird is a cockatoo, it will raise its crest and puff itself up during display. This display is normal and is usually accompanied by loud screeching, as well as hostility to anyone perceived as a rival entering his territory.

Screaming and Excessive Vocalization

Birds that want to breed will call out for a mate as long as it takes to get a mate to come around. In the case of a parrot living by itself in a home, that could be a very long time. As the frustration of not having a mate increases, so does the screaming, which can be persistent.

This Amazon parrot is in "full display" mode and will probably bite if someone tries to pick him up.

Biting

Hormonal parrots can be unpredictable, and even a bird that has never previously bitten may give you a nicely placed chomp. Hormonal reasons for biting include defending territory, defending a mate (biting someone to get them away from you or biting you so that you get away from someone else), and general excitement. The best way to prevent a bite is to avoid it. An Amazon parrot with its irises wildly pinning in and out, a cockatoo that's screaming and displaying, or a cockatiel that's crouched low and hissing are not birds that are going to step up politely onto your hand. Wait until your bird is having a calm moment to interact with it.

Unwarranted Aggression

Sometimes hormonal birds don't bite just when interacted with, but will actively locate their victim for an attack. This includes parrots that come down from their cage tops or perches and pursue a victim on foot, or dive-bomb and bite a victim's head and face (if the bird is able to fly). The reason for this is chiefly territorial. Someone who poses a threat (your spouse, friend, child, etc.) needs to be scared away from your parrot's little utopia, where you and it will live together forever, alone and happy.

Egg Laying

Female parrots can lay eggs without the presence of a male, just like chickens, and will defend these infertile eggs fiercely. Allow such a female to sit on her egg for two or three days, then take it away from her while she's distracted. Use a thick glove or towel to remove the egg, and take it to a place where she can't see it. Shortly after the egg is gone she should go back to behaving like her usual self.

Getting a Hold on the Hormones

Because seasonal hormones are triggered by external stimuli, removing the stimuli should take the hormonal behavior down a notch. There are other factors to consider as well—nutrition, your social interaction with the bird, the family dynamics, and so on. The following are a few things that should help to make your bird "livable" during a hormonal period.

1. Decrease the amount of light your parrot receives in every 24-hour period. Parrots are sensitive to photo periods and experience a hormone surge in the springtime when the days are longer than the nights, so artificially decreasing the amount of light that your parrot gets should "trick" the bird's hormones into subsiding. A parrot's hormones are usually in full swing by the time daylight is 12 to 14 hours long. Around the time that you turn your clocks ahead, make sure that your parrot only receives 9 to 10 hours of light a day (natural or artificial).

Go Organic

The pesticides used on foods aren't just bad for us to eat, but are very dangerous for birds, which have systems far smaller and more sensitive than ours. Pesticides can affect hormone levels and cause behavioral issues. Use organic vegetables and fruit when you can.

If your parrot lives in a central part of the house, you may have to put the bird into a comfortable sleeping cage in a darkened room with blackout shades on the windows, and cover the cage partially with a dark cloth. This cage should be used only for sleeping, and there should always be food and water in it. When the clocks roll back in the fall, you can resume your normal routine, but by this time your bird might be used to sleeping in the other cage and will want to continue doing so.

The one problem I've encountered with this method, which is proven and effective, is that it creates a conflict for working families who are gone all day. The parrot usually gets all of its human attention in the mornings, before work, and in the evenings, around dinner time and before bedtime. That gives the bird

Is My Bird a Boy or a Girl?

Most species of companion birds are monomorphic, meaning that there's no visual difference between the sexes. The most obvious exception is the eclectus parrots, a dimorphic species whose male is bright green and whose female is bright red and purple. For many years, aviculturists had no luck breeding these birds because they insisted on pairing up the greens with the greens and the reds with the reds!

Some of the other companion birds, like many of the keets and the cockatiels, are sexually dimorphic, with clear visual differences between the sexes, but outside of those birds, gender is anyone's guess. Experienced bird keepers can often tell a mature monomorphic male from a mature female by the shape of the head and beak, subtle differences in coloring, the shape of the hips, and differences in behavior, but these characteristics can be deceiving.

Most companion parrots make loving, loyal pals no matter the gender. There are some behavioral differences between the sexes in most species, but not enough to make it worth your while to select a parrot with a particular gender in mind. Just choose a bird that you bond with, an individual that seems to like you as much as you like it. If you really want to know your bird's gender, there's an easy, painless DNA test that uses a blood or feather sample to accurately confirm whether your feathered pal is a boy or a girl.

much more than ten hours of light a day. There's no easy remedy for this conflict. Something has to change in the human schedule, because giving the parrot less attention will create more behavioral problems than an extended photo period will.

Outside Influences on Behavior Problems

2. Make sure your hormonal bird is getting the proper nutrients, especially calcium if it is a female. A bird that's eating a diet poor in nutrients is bound to have hormonal imbalance, which means trouble for its owner. Feed your bird as well as you feed yourself.

To Breed or Not to Breed?

At the time of this writing there are more parrots in sanctuaries and foster homes than in the entire history of bird keeping. These are parrots that were given up by their owners because the bird was too loud, too aggressive, too messy. Or, perhaps, the bird wasn't affectionate enough, not talkative enough, simply a disappointment to its owners. Often, parrots are given up because the owner is moving, getting married, having a baby, going to college, or just got bored of this pet and moved on to another. Whatever the reason, there are too many birds being bred and not enough permanent homes for them.

Unless you want to join a consortium that's dedicated to breeding an endangered species, it might be a good idea to reconsider the decision to breed your bird, especially if it's a common species. Aviculture is best left to the professionals who have the resources and know-how to properly care for their birds. Breeding birds on a small scale costs more money than it makes, and it endangers the lives of the breeding birds, which are at risk for reproductive disorders as well as bird-on-bird aggression from an unpredictable mate. If breeding birds is an endeavor that you think you'd like to try, consult other breeders first, do your research, and create a plan, including known and potential costs, time factors, and legitimate placement of the babies.

No, let me revise that—feed your bird better than you feed yourself.

3. Don't give your hormonal bird a chance to bite you in the first place. This is common sense—if you wag your finger in an Amazon's face while he is displaying, you're going to lose part of it. Learn your bird's "biting body language" and get out of the way when the bird is on the war path.

4. Discourage cage territoriality. A hormonal bird will defend its cage against interlopers, a situation that may become quite a problem if the bird is hostile and fearless. If you see that your bird is more hostile around its cage, which is natural around breeding time, remove it from the cage with a dowel or perch and take it to a neutral room for playtime.

Eating Well and the Picky Parrot

Parrot nutrition is a much-debated topic, with the various sides standing staunchly in favor of their position, with little flexibility. I can only offer you the diet that works for my birds and my clients' birds, the diet that I've developed from years of personal experience and the experience of other bird guardians I know and respect. The diet I propose makes sense, is easy to offer, and will optimize your bird's nourishment if you follow it daily.

Why is nutrition so important for behavioral issues? A bird that's lacking in nutrients is more prone to illness, and an ill bird is not going to be a pleasure to

Even picky parrots should be encouraged to eat healthy foods.

live with. An undernourished parrot is also more likely to die far earlier than its expected life span, a tragic and common consequence of malnutrition.

Most parrots in the wild eat a wide variety of food; some are reported to eat more than 75 different types of plant material. How is it possible to replicate a diet like that? Well, it's not possible, even if you tried. Parrots eat only what's in season, and some of them are opportunistic, feeding on farmland and destroying crops. Some will eat bugs if they can catch them, and some occasionally rely on other types of animals to provide a meal. Some regularly eat mineral-rich clay from rainforest cliffs, and some live primarily on only one or two types of plant material. Basically, to really feed your parrot the way it should be fed, you would have to research its exact diet in its natural habitat and replicate it. Good luck.

So, we have to feed our parrots using the resources at hand. Here's a list of the variety of good foods and the ratio in which you should be feeding them:

Seed

Birdseed has gotten a bad rap in the last few years. True, it is not as nutrient dense as some other foods, but there are some birds, like the parakeet and the cockatiel, that eat seed in the wild as the staple of their diet. Some of what they eat is young seed and has more nutrients than dry seed, but they eat their fair share of mature seeds as well. It's also true that some birds, such as rainforest dwellers, never, ever eat the kinds of seeds typically available in a seed mix.

Seed should not be the base of your parrot's diet, but should be offered as a part of a well-rounded nutritional plan. Birds that eat only seed and water

Seed and pellets make up only part of a good, balanced diet.

don't live a fifth of their life expectancy, and they succumb easily to malnutrition and related diseases. Seed should comprise approximately 20 percent of your parrot's total diet.

Pellets

Pellets are at the top of the bird nutrition debate. One camp says feed pellets and nothing else, and the other says don't feed pellets at all. The reality of pellets is that they are not nutritionally complete for every bird, have not been scientifically tested on every species, and some varieties have been proven to eventually cause liver and kidney dysfunction in birds that live solely on a diet of pellets and water. The reality of seeds is the same. So what to do? Well, the seed companies had a good idea

Peanuts are relished and are fun to eat, but offer them in strict moderation.

when they began introducing pellets into seed mixes. Both pellets and seed are fine to feed if the rest of the diet is nutritious and various. My birds eat and relish both. Some birds will pick out the seeds in the mix and leave the pellets behind, so watch that the seed intake doesn't become excessive. Pellets can comprise 10 to 20 percent of the total diet.

Fruits and Vegetables

Fresh produce is wonderful for your bird and offers it a lot of important vitamins and minerals.

Fresh produce is essential to your parrot's health – and he'll love it too!

Unfortunately, mass-produced fruits and veggies are typically grown in soil where the nutrients have been used up over many years of crops. Also, the various pesticides, fungicides, and fertilizers used on our produce can make it toxic (or at least not very good) for our parrots. Feed organically grown produce when possible, or grow your own.

Dark orange and dark green vegetables and fruit are the best for your bird because they are nutrient dense and are rich in vitamin A, which your bird needs to maintain a healthy respiratory system.

Make sure to remove all fruit within a few hours of feeding it—it can spoil, or attract "fruit flies," pesky little flying things that are tough to get rid of. Cooked veggies should also be removed within a few hours if you live in a warm climate. Sprouted beans and seeds

Foods That are Good for Your Bird

Vegetables	Fruits
yams (cooked) spinach	grapes
broccoli	figs
kale	apples
collard greens	apricots
spinach	
celery	watermelon
jalapenos	cantaloupe
green pepper	bananas
red pepper	cherries
yellow pepper	oranges
beet tops	peaches
pumpkin	plums
zucchini	
watercress	papaya
peas	mango
corn	kiwi
green beans	honeydew
endive	berries
dandelion	grapefruit
asparagus	
beets (raw or cooked)	pineapple
carrots (raw or cooked)	pear
brussels sprouts	
mustard greens	
yellow squash	
chard	

are incredibly nutritious and most birds love them. You can buy a sprouting kit or buy the sprouts from your local farmer's market. Fresh produce should comprise 40 to 50 percent of your bird's total diet.

Cooked Foods

Some people cook specifically for their birds, using nutritious, easily digestible foods that their parrot

Important Vitamins and Minerals for Well-Behaved Birds

Vitamin A: Companion parrots are very prone to vitamin A deficiency because they need more of it than we do (by weight) and the things that they typically eat are poor in it. Feed fruits and vegetables that are orange or very green.

Vitamin D3: Birds synthesize this vitamin naturally when the sunlight shines on their feathers. Allowing your bird to have some time in the sun (not through a window, though) or shining wide-spectrum bird lamps on the bird's cage should be enough to prevent a D3 deficiency.

Calcium: Some birds, such as African grey parrots and certain Amazons, are prone to calcium deficiency, as are birds laying eggs. Provide a lot of dark green vegetables, as well as a calcium block. Some birds may need a calcium supplement.

loves. Parrots tend to like warm foods a lot, especially if they were handfed as babies. Beans and rice, whole wheat macaroni and soy cheese, and birdy corn bread are among the recipes I make for my birds. I add veggies, liquid vitamins, calcium powder, dried fruit, pellets, and anything else I have in the house that's good for the birds. Cooked foods can comprise 20 to 30 percent of your parrot's diet.

Juices

Freshly squeezed juices are terrific for your parrot, and you can share them, too. I make a health shake for myself every morning, and I started sharing it with my African grey, who loves to drink out of a glass.

Clean Water

Water quality is very important for a bird's health. Soupy water into which your bird has tossed food, toys, and...well, used as a toilet, is not the ideal beverage. Bacteria grow easily in this kind of "poop soup" and can make your bird very ill. Change your bird's water as many times a day as you can, but at least twice. Using a bacteria inhibitor or grapefruit seed extract (found at health food stores) will help cut down on the things swimming in your bird's water dish. The water dish should be made of stainless steel, and you should have two—one that's being used and one that's soaking in bleach and scrubbed for use the next day. Also, if you can, use only bottled or purified water (not distilled); tap water can contain chlorine and organisms that can harm your bird.

When he started begging to share my shake each morning, I got wise and started making him his own, complete with calcium powder and an extra mineral complex. The rest of the shake includes orange juice, soy milk, protein powder, liquid minerals and vitamins, powdered vitamin C, aloe juice, flax seed oil, acidophilus, and a banana. Juices and shakes can comprise 5 to 10 percent of your bird's total diet.

Table Foods

Your parrot can eat just about anything that you eat. With the exception of chocolate, avocado, rhubarb, alcohol, and salty, sugary, and fatty foods, your bird can eat everything on your plate. Share your meals and be persistent if your bird is reluctant to try new foods—simply keep offering them and your bird's

Offering clean water is essential to your bird's health.

curiosity will get the best of it. It might seem like cannibalism, but your parrot might even enjoy some turkey or chicken, and larger parrots will relish a chicken bone. Don't forget to bring a "birdy bag" home with you when you go out to eat. Table foods can comprise 10 to 15 percent of your bird's total diet.

A Dietary Plan

The key to feeding your parrot well is variety, variety, variety. Some parrots are set in their ways and refuse to eat the things that you know are good for them. But parrots are curious creatures and will eventually taste (or at least explore) a food if you keep offering it. It shouldn't take more than two weeks of offering a specific food before your parrot decides to figure out whether it likes the new food or not. Some parrot guardians get discouraged and stop offering a food after two or three tries. Don't give up! Yes, it's a waste of food at first, but it will pay off in the long run with fewer veterinary bills. Parrots, like us, have a preference for certain items and distaste for others. Your bird may not ever try a specific food, so if it hasn't eaten the yams in a few weeks, give up on them for a while or try offering them in a different form: cooked, grated, mashed, and so on.

Parrots eat when they are hungry (unless they're eating out of boredom, but that's another situation altogether). Feeding a complete diet means offering the most nutritious foods when your parrot is hungriest. Birds generally feed just after dawn, and then feed again just before dusk. You can capitalize on these "hungry" times by feeding the items you would like your bird to eat when it is most likely to do so.

For example, in the mornings offer a large dish or two with at least four different vegetables and two or three types of fruit—vegetables are better for your bird because they contain less sugar, though some fruits are very high in good nutrients and should not be overlooked. Vary the textures of the foods by alternately shredding, chopping, and cooking the produce, though some foods are fun to eat whole, like an ear of corn, a carrot, and grapes. Also offer some nutritious cooked food at this meal, as well as a few tablespoons of seed and pellets—less or more depending on the size of the bird. Some sips of juice or a shake is also great in the morning. Whole wheat bread or whole wheat crackers spread thinly with peanut butter is appreciated, as is yogurt (which my African grey

Vitamin and Mineral Supplements

Some people say that if you feed your bird well enough, it shouldn't need a vitamin or mineral supplement. Well, if that means that I have to recreate its diet in its natural habitat, I'd better supplement my birds' diet. I use a vitamin powder as well as a calcium liquid in the water; I also use a mineral powder and a calcium powder on soft foods. Twice a week I use a probiotic powder (a powder made up of beneficial organisms) in the water instead of the other supplements and I change the water two or three times on those days.

Obesity

Obesity is a common problem in many companion birds and can lead to serious health issues and even death. Feeding too much seed is often the cause of obesity in birds, as is lack of proper exercise. Obesity leads to tumors, gout, and sometimes sudden death.

loves), and one or two almonds or other nuts (don't overfeed peanuts, please).

In the evening, offer sprouts, very well-done chopped hardboiled or scrambled egg (including the shell), pieces of well-done chicken or fish, a small piece of low-fat cheese or soy cheese, table foods, and other fruits and veggies—the more the better. If your bird is eating these items, there's no need to include seed in this meal—the bird has already had its seed quota for the day, and it is better off eating more nutritious stuff. Don't ever take the seed and pellet cup away, though. Your bird should have something available to eat at all times. Remember, soft and fresh foods spoil easily, so remove them a few hours after you offer them.

If you're home during the day, a three-meal plan is even better. The "lunch" meal can consist of sprouted beans and seeds, cooked beans and peas, and anything else your bird likes, with the exception of seed. Birds also like to eat when their "flock" eats, so if you can set a place for your bird near the dining table, it will be more likely to consume more of the "good stuff."

Please, whatever you do, don't starve your bird. Make sure it's eating something in each meal. Smaller birds can actually die from missing too many consecutive meals. Snacks such as air-popped popcorn and rice cakes make a good between-meal snack

Home Tweet Home

Your parrot's cage should be a safe haven, not a prison. All birds need a cage, but that doesn't mean that the bird should be locked in it all day. The cage should be as large as your budget and space can afford, and if you can build an aviary or habitat, that's even better. A cage where the bird can flap its wings and spread them out and turn around is inadequate, despite what the old literature says. Birds are animals of boundless space, and they become neurotic when confined. An animal that is meant to fly will not be happy in a cage where it can only spread its wings and turn around. It's true that there are birds that won't come out of the cage, no matter what the guardian does; these birds seem to "love" the cage, but that's not the truth. This is a bird that is so terrified that it clings to the cage for dear life—not the picture of a well-adjusted animal.

A parrot that lives in a cage that's too small for it will not be easily tamed or trained. Proper housing is just as important as good nutrition and health care. The cage should have a large door

Birds become neurotic when confined for too long.

that swings down or to the side to open, not one that slides up and down guillotine-style. This way the bird can come out of the cage on its own when you open the door, safely, without having to be violently fished out for every training session.

Time outside the cage is essential for most parrots.

The cage should have a playpen on top where the bird can go to play on its own without having bars surrounding it. There's a great psychological benefit for a bird that has a safe place to play without feeling confined. Look for a cage with both vertical and horizontal bars, and one without complicated scrollwork where the bird can catch a toe. Horizontally rectangular cages are better than square cages, and square cages are better than round ones.

The cage is not a place to put the bird when it's being given a "time out," nor is it the place to put your bird when you want it to be quiet. The cage is the bird's home and it should be allowed to do all the things you would do in your own home: talk, rest, sleep, bathe, eat, play, groom itself, toss food around (you do that, don't you?), and so on. Screaming in or on top of the cage at certain times of day is normal, and shouldn't be discouraged or punished, even though it can seem like a "problem" behavior.

Cage Placement and Behavior

Cage placement can directly affect a parrot's behavior. Here's a list of the do's and don'ts of cage placement:

* Do place the cage in a well-trafficked area of the home. Birds that are confined to a back bedroom or a garage will suffer tremendous loneliness, and behavioral problems are bound to ensue. A family room, television room, or living room is ideal—the place where you spend most of your time and where there's likely to be family activity. The bedroom, a child's room, a hallway, the bathroom, and the kitchen are not good places for the cage.

* Do place the cage in a corner or against a wall. A bird feels safe if there's a blocked corner to retreat to when it feels insecure or wants to nap. Never place the cage in the center of a room unless you cover a third of it with a thick cloth or other safe material.

* Don't place the cage directly next to a window. Instead, place it near the window or place half of the cage against the window with the other half along a wall. The heat from the sun may be overcome the bird if the window is sunny, and the presence of predators outside (neighborhood dogs and cats, raccoons, cars passing by, and hawks flying overhead) is scary to a bird, which needs to be able to retreat to a safe place in the cage. A bird that's on the lookout for predators all day long with no place to go when it sees one is not going to be a well-behaved bird, but a tired and cranky one.

* Don't place the cage on the floor, unless it comes elevated on legs. A bird that's too low to the ground is going to be very insecure, especially if there are dogs and cats in the home. Place the cage on a stand or a piece of furniture. Contrary to other viewpoints, it's okay if the cage is high enough for the bird to be above your head when it's on the top perch or cage-top playpen. The higher a bird is, the

more secure it feels—it has a better view of the world and can make sure there are no predators in its midst.

✳ Do find a good place for the cage and keep it there. Moving the bird's cage around as if it's a couch will be disturbing and can create behavioral issues.

What's Outside the Cage?

Very often I have clients whose birds have developed sudden behavioral problems due to something outside the cage within the bird's sight. Maybe the neighbors have just put in one of those movement-sensitive lights that switch off and on all night, and your bird is near a window. Maybe mice have gotten into your home and scuttle around at night, disturbing your bird. Maybe you've changed your hair color, shaved off your beard, or have gotten a new piece of art, a new kitten, a disco ball. Whatever the case, try to see the world as your bird sees it—what's new in its vicinity that could possibly be disturbing?

The cage should be a safe haven, not a prison.

New carpeting and freshly painted walls or stucco ceilings can be toxic for your bird, whose respiratory system is very sensitive. These items can create strange behavior in a bird, which may pluck, bite, or behave a little like it's drunk or high. Air out a newly carpeted or painted room for a couple of months before a bird begins to reside there.

Proper Grooming

Grooming is a natural behavior that parrots do for themselves without human aid. They preen each feather every day to make sure it's clean, in the right place, and that each strand comprising the feather is zipped tightly to the next. Feathers are integral to a bird's well-being. They keep a bird insulated from heat and cold, keep it dry in a rainstorm, and allow for flight. Preening helps new feathers to come in, and, in some species, breaks the powder-down feathers that grow close to

A healthy parrot will groom itself several times daily.

the skin so that the powder can keep the feathers clean and supple. Most species of parrots have a "preen gland" at the base of their tail that secretes an oil that the bird rubs on its feathers during preening.

When we talk about grooming in the bird world, we aren't talking about preening but about clipping a bird's wings and toenails and offering regular bathing. An improperly groomed parrot is a likely candidate for problem behaviors.

Most people who live with companion parrots in their home clip their bird's wings so that it can't fly away or injure itself by flying into objects inside the house. Personally, I'm an advocate of allowing birds to fly in a safe space built specifically with flying in mind, but the average household, where most companion

This blue and gold macaw has a neat, sufficient clip, as you can see by the missing flight feathers on the end of its wing.

birds live, holds too many dangers to allow free-wielding flight. Clipping a bird's wings does not hurt it physically, but an improper clip can leave sharp edges on the ends of the wing feathers, which can poke into the bird's side and cause plucking to begin.

Dive-bombing family members, hiding, and general dangerous mischief are often typical of a fully flighted bird when it begins to have a hormone surge in the springtime. I know of Amazons, conures, and macaws that have flown into an interloper's face (that is, a spouse, guest, or child) to bite the person ferociously. This type of behavior is easily quelled by clipping the wings. This doesn't mean that the wings should not be allowed to grow out again, which they will do during the next molt, but it does mean that caution should be taken with a bird that is fearless and territorial enough to attack a creature 100 times its size.

Toenails should be blunted so that it's a pleasant experience to play with the bird, not a painful one. If you cut your bird's toenails yourself, you can avoid the trauma of restraining your bird by clipping only one toenail a day with a regular nail clipper, and only taking off the very tip so that the nail doesn't bleed. I like to catch my birds by surprise when I'm playing with them—one little snip and the operation is over until the next day. No drama or trauma needed. If you're too scared or squeamish to do it yourself, your avian veterinarian will be happy to oblige.

Bathing is important for a bird's skin and feather condition. Most birds will bathe themselves in the water dish or in the sink or shower when you're running the water. Some will love to be misted or even soaked in a shower from a hose. You can bathe your bird every day in warm weather, and a couple of times a week in colder weather; however, if your bird loves to bathe, let it do so whenever it wants. Bathing relieves itchy dry skin, which can lead to feather chewing and plucking. A bird that won't bathe can be enticed to do so with a shallow dish of water in its cage; try allowing it to sit near flowing water (like a sink) or watch you shower. Misting is also good, but do so gently with a bird that's water-phobic for the moment.

This African grey enjoys a shower – make sure your bird will tolerate such bathing before you offer this type of bath.

Bathing is important for your bird's skin and feathers.

Where Did Your Parrot Come From?

Where your parrot came from is an important factor in figuring out why it has become entrenched in one or more problem behaviors. A bird's rearing and early life can tell you a lot about its behavior. For most people, their bird's origin is a mystery. That's okay. There are only four basic "types" of companion birds: wild caught, parent raised, bred in captivity, and secondhand.

Wild-Caught Parrots

The wild-caught parrot is one that grew up in the wild (or was collected as a nestling out of a nesting hole) and was caught and brought into captivity. You will not find a wild-caught parrot to purchase unless the bird was recently smuggled or has been in the United States since before the early 1990s, when the CITES act eliminated the importation of birds in the US. Bird traders, brokers, and breeders quickly realized the crisis they had on their hands, and they began collecting breeding stock to make sure that there would be enough parrots to meet the demand of the pet trade. Consequently, some parrots are more common in captivity than they are in the wild, and some aren't available in the US anymore but are plentiful in captivity on other continents.

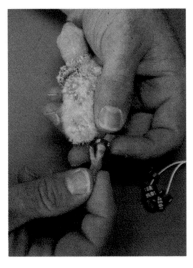

Most domestically bred baby birds will have a closed band placed on the leg as a hatchling. Here, a three-week-old Sun Conure receives a band.

Most wild-caught parrots that aren't in breeding situations are already tame or semi-tame and have been living in homes for the past decade or more. Most states now have regulations requiring that all domestically bred babies be closed banded—a ring with no opening is placed on the hatchling's leg when it's just a few days old and remains on its leg indefinitely, or until an avian veterinarian removes it with a special tool (never try to remove it yourself or risk breaking your bird's leg). Wild-caught parrots can be recognized by an open band on the leg, one that was clamped on, though many of these birds have had the band removed.

At this point, the behavior of a wild-caught bird isn't going to be much different than that of a parent-raised bird. Wild-caught birds currently available as companions have had plenty of time to get used to life with humans, and whether or not the birds are socialized and tame is completely dependant upon the taming and training they received from previous owners.

Parent-Raised Birds
Parent-raised birds are bred in captivity but are not pulled out of the nest by the breeder to be handfed; instead, they are left with the parents for rearing. Parent-raised birds are often bigger than their handfed counterparts and have better immune systems, though they are not socialized to humans and will need taming and training.

Some species, such as the parakeet and the cockatiel, can be handled while still under parental care. It's common practice for breeders to open the nest once or twice a day and gently handle the babies. These birds get the best of both worlds. They are a little more skittish than hand-reared birds, but are more quickly and easily befriended.

"Gimme, Gimme!" This baby Cockatoo is being handfed by its human guardians.

Hand-Reared Parrots
Hand-reared parrots are pulled from their parent's nest between the ages of two and three weeks. Some breeders pull the eggs from the parents and keep them warm in specially designed incubators. Hand-reared parrots are imprinted on humans and don't need taming because they

grow up knowing only a human as caretaker and nurturer. A hand-reared parrot can certainly be ignored and abused into reverting to an untamed state, but if socialized and treated properly, it can stay sweet and friendly during its entire life.

Behavioral problems occur in hand-reared birds because of a slip on the part of its guardians. This is an attentive bird that knows only the social structure and habits of humans, and it looks to its human friends for every aspect of its life to be tended to, from interaction to proper housing. When something is awry, the hand-reared parrot notices right away and reacts. Often that reaction is perceived as negative to the humans around it, who misinterpret the behavior as naughtiness, when it's actually a cry for help.

The Secondhand Parrot

The secondhand parrot is probably the worst off of the lot. This is a bird that is in a second, third, or tenth home and has been so grossly misunderstood that most people are quick to give up on it. This bird only wants to be part of things, to be loved and respected. However, it's loud, plucked, messy, hostile, ill, or a combination of these things, and that's much more than the average bird owner can bear.

If you've inherited or adopted a secondhand bird, take heart—there is hope. You aren't the one that instilled these problem behaviors, so you just might be the one to help the bird substitute them for more positive activities. This isn't a bad bird. It's just a misunderstood bird, and it can change for the better

Second-hand birds can make great companions when introduced into a loving home.

to lead a happy, social life in a human home without being shuffled along again.

Developing a Plan

When I consult with my bird clients about remedies for their parrot's "monster" behavior, the behavior only changes when they actually put what I propose into action, which is usually a combination of things, from changing the bird's environment and diet, to the guardians changing their own behavior around the bird. Changing these things isn't always easy. For example, if a bird needs a larger cage, the guardians may claim not to have the space or money to acquire one. What then? If a larger cage is part of the plan to remedy a behavioral problem, the plan will not work without it. In most cases, no one change will eliminate problem behavior, but a system of changes usually will.

Checklist for Good Health

1. Do you view your bird as an individual and give it the dignity and respect you would give a good friend?

2. Do you have an avian veterinarian? If not, find the phone number of one in your area as soon as possible.

3. Make a list of what your bird eats on a daily basis. If there are only one or two items on the list, revise your bird's nutritional plan. The more variety the better.

4. Is your bird's water clean right now? How often do you change it and wash the water dish?

5. Check the size, type, and placement of your parrot's cage. Is it big enough? Is it in a place where your bird gets enough social interaction and feels secure?

6. Is your bird properly groomed? How long are its toenails? Is its beak in good condition? How often do you mist it with clean, warm water?

7. If your bird is behaving strangely, have you checked for anything new in its immediate environment?

Your
Bird's
Secret Life

Most of what you need to get along with your bird comes from simply understanding why it does what it does and then accommodating your behavior to "manipulate" your bird's behavior. This isn't that far off from how we "train" children or the other people around us. Every interaction we have is a dance of reward/no-reward, and that's how we learn which actions work for us and which do not. The same goes for birds.

Understanding Your Bird's Instincts

Instincts are essentially defined as unconscious acts.

Birds are highly instinctual creatures that aren't "out to get you." They just want to be birds.

Because your bird is a wild animal, it does many things for no other reason than that it is programmed to do them. A bird doesn't take actions to aid you in your daily life or to deliberately hurt you; it is just acting on its natural programming. The bird, like other animals (including us), has one primary purpose: to stay alive. Its secondary purpose is to procreate (which is why it needs to stay alive). Everything it does is geared toward these two drives.

This might make the companion bird sound quite mechanical. But, when you think about all of the complicated things a bird has to do to stay alive and procreate, including actions we don't think of as being related to those intentions—such as playing, talking, or bonding to an organism outside of its species—the bird becomes a complex organism, similar to ourselves.

Normal Birdy Behaviors

Many of a bird's instinctual behaviors are considered "problem" behaviors, because they are really not programmed to live in the average household setting. Some of the larger parrots quickly prove themselves to be nuisances to their guardians just by behaving the way a parrot is supposed to behave. One person's angelic parrot is another person's nightmare.

Chewing is a normal and healthy part of your bird's life. This blue-crowned conure enjoys chewing his wooden toy.

There are some behaviors inherent in a companion bird that are not going to change. If these behaviors are squelched, a truly unhappy, neurotic beast is likely to result. The following are some behaviors that you're going to have to live with:

Chewing

Most birds are expert demolitionists. Chewing is a natural behavior that allows a parrot to exert energy and keep its beak trimmed; in some cases, chewing is also part of the breeding cycle. You are not going to get a parrot to stop chewing, but you can choose what your parrot is allowed to chew on. Offer soft wood toys, hard woods, branches with the bark still attached, leather, cardboard, paper, rope, and other safe chewing materials. Don't get angry at a bird that consistently chews up its perches; that's what the beak is designed to do.

Birds that aren't allowed some self-direction can become habitual pluckers, like this blue and gold macaw.

Screaming and Other Disturbing Sounds

Most parrots kick up a racket at dawn and just before dusk. This is part of how parrots communicate with other parrots, and it is going to be a difficult, if not impossible, behavior to quell. Instead of letting it drive you crazy, especially if you have a loud bird like a cockatoo or a macaw, plan for the vocalizations and accept them as something that's part of living with a parrot. Intermittent screaming and vocalizations will also happen during the day, but all-day screaming is not normal and should be addressed.

Talking

Parrots in the wild do not talk (mimic human language, that is) but they do learn the language of their flock. In a home setting, a parrot is a member of a different kind of flock and will, if it has the capacity, make the effort to learn its flock's language. Birds use talking and other human sounds to communicate with the humans around them, and though they sometimes misunderstand what the sounds mean (mimicking a microwave beeping is not going to get a human to come running to a parrot), they are often able to associate words and sounds with an action and are able to communicate what they want with their humans, just as they would to their bird friends in the wild.

Flying

Flying isn't unique to birds, but it is unique to commonly kept companion animals, and it presents a unique problem in the average household. It's common to clip a bird's wings to prevent it from flying, and though that's done to keep a bird safe in a home, it also removes the bird's primary fear response. In cases where the guardians aren't sensitive to the bird's needs, this lack of a fear response often leads to behaviors such as biting, screaming, and plucking. Some people do allow their birds to fly inside and have some self-direction, but those birds are far more prone to flying away or becoming injured than are their clipped counterparts. The only real remedy for this dilemma is to create a safe place for the bird to fly and still remain a companion. Most people don't have the facilities for such a place or are unwilling to change the way their bird is housed, so most birds are going to remain clipped for their entire lives. A clipped bird can indeed lead a fulfilled life if it is cared for properly and has the type of interaction it needs to remain emotionally healthy. "Problem" birds, those that are dive-bombing or viciously biting family members, should be clipped in order give behavior modification a chance.

Paper Shredding

Many parrots like to shred and play with paper. This is normal and shouldn't be discouraged. It gives the parrot something to do, and in some cases, like the peach-faced and eye-ringed lovebirds, it is part of nesting behavior. Remove the paper from lovebirds if breeding is a problem, such as with a hen that is prone to egg-binding.

Display

When springtime comes, some male parrots will make a big show of themselves, strutting around making a lot of noise and displaying their feathers. This is normal, albeit loud and sometimes dangerous for the human who gets in the way.

Nail Biting

Some birds pick at their nails and feet, which is a normal part of grooming. There's only cause for concern when the bird begins to pick the flesh on the feet and causes bleeding.

Flock Behavior?

Many dog and cat owners claim that their pet runs the show in their home; the dog is the king of the house and the cat is the queen of the whole block. This may seem to be the case, but in reality dogs and cats have instinctual programming that says otherwise. Sure, if the dog and cat owners don't enforce any rules, the animal may run the place, but this doesn't happen in the majority of households. Just watch Fluffy stop using the litter box and Fido start doing his doggie "business" in the owner's bed, and see how fast the tables turn. Dogs understand that a family (a pack) involves a hierarchy, and that, in general, the humans are alpha, the leaders of the

Birds of a feather may seem to flock together, but that's not necessarily the case. Is there a leader among these lovebirds? Probably not.

pack. Cats are programmed to be solitary animals, but once introduced into a family, become dependant on them (well, most cats, anyway!). There are some rogue dogs that do take over a household, but that behavior is not tolerated for long.

Parrots don't have this kind of "pack" programming, and though it seems as if they're all flocking animals, most of them are not. The word flock implies a relationship between the members of the flock, that there's a leader, a sentinel, and so on. Birds of a feather do flock together, but they interact less in the way that pack animals do and more in the way that fish school together. Yes, birds do fly together in remarkable synchronicity, but fish school together in the same way. Does this mean that there's one fish leader leading the hundreds of other minnows to food or safety?

Parrots, like fish, are prey animals. Small parrots, like the budgie, occur in flocks of hundreds, a visually confusing mass for a predator. All the motion, lines, and colors moving in a sometimes chaotic mass make it difficult for a hawk to set its sights on one budgie as a target. Birds like these hang out together because there's safety in numbers, and, remember, a parrot's primary purpose is to stay alive. A parrot's secondary purpose is to procreate, which is another reason why parrots hang out together. The same can be said for other parrots that hang out in large groups, such as cockatoos, grey parrots, and some conures. In parrot groups, utility is valued over hierarchy.

Some parrots, like the quaker parakeet, do live in communities and build large, shared nests. Because the birds watch out for predators and help with nesting (procreation), it serves them well to "flock," though there is no leader as such. Other parrots, like the large macaws, do not exhibit this kind of communal behavior. They hang out in couples and small groups. When people see them in the wild congregated by the dozens on a fruiting tree, they may seem like a "flock" of parrots, but what they really are is a bunch of animals of the same species feeding in the same place, the way we humans feed at a restaurant buffet. A friend of mine who lives with more than 100 free-flighted macaws makes the point that it might seem like humans in a restaurant are "flocking," but really we're just there in our small groups; we eat and then leave without a lot of interaction with the others.

The majority of interaction a parrot has with other parrots is with its mate and its chicks. Most parrots are monogamous, and though there are little infidelities here and there, they mate for life. A parrot living in a home gets most of its interaction from the humans it lives with. It stands to reason that a sexually mature parrot may choose one person in the home to be its one and only love. Why should it try to be a member of an artificial flock, especially when it's not going to be the leader?

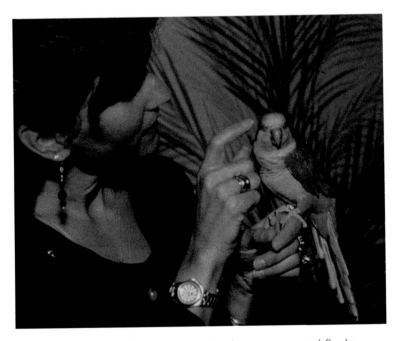

Wild Quaker parakeets hang out in large communal flocks, but captive bred Quakers make wonderful single-bird companions.

The View From Above

Parrots have a natural tendency to want to perch in a high place. A high spot is a good vantage point to watch for predators. It was previously thought that a bird sitting in a high place in a home is trying to be dominant over its human guardians. Yes, it is difficult to get a bird down from a high spot, but it is being no more dominant than a Boy Scout in a lookout in a tree house. It does sometimes feel like the bird is laughing up there, saying, "Ha, ha, you can't get me! I'm the leader of this flock!" What's really going on is more like, "Hey, I've found a nice place to sit where I can see everything, and it has the advantage that you can't get me and put me back into the cage." Your bird is no dummy.

Instead of the household decree stating, "My parrot must obey me," perhaps it should be, "Why can't we all just get along?" A parrot is a highly social animal, and it will want to interact with the humans around it, but not at the expense of being viewed as somehow inferior to everyone else. Try to remember that you are not a true flock, but a group of individuals (some with feathers and some without) with needs, desires, and basic requirements to remain happy and fulfilled.

Dominance

The myth of the parrot "flock" gave birth to the myth of parrot dominance. Parrots are simply not programmed to be dominant over humans. Dominance implies that one individual takes on the responsibility for being dominant over the other, shaping the way the other lives its life. It's true that a jealous fit among parrots may look like one is dominating the other, but what's really going on is a parrot defending its secondary purpose, to procreate. Male and female parrots have different roles in nesting and raising chicks; when one mate insists that the other go back inside the nest to tend to the chicks, that bird is not dominating the other, but is looking out for the interests of its own genes.

When your parrot bites you or tries to shoo you away from its body or cage, the bird is not trying to dominate you; it simply wants to be left alone at the moment, or is afraid, not feeling well, and so on. Parrots are self-directed creatures that do not handle authority well. A guardian that tries to be less of an authority and more of a friend is going to have a "better behaved" parrot than someone who insists on making the bird behave a certain way on the spot. Praise, not dominance, works to shape parrot behavior.

Practical Solutions to Outta Control Problems

In This Chapter You'll Learn:

✳ How to train yourself to help your bird

✳ What to do about excessive vocalization

✳ How to handle biting

✳ Why Polly plucks

Get out your Sherlock Holmes hat and magnifying glass; we're going to get to the root of your bird's problem, dig it out, and dispose of it— or at least reverse it as much as possible. Life with your bird shouldn't be just bearable, but mutually rewarding and satisfying. The solutions to changing your "monster" back into a friend are on the way.

When Is a Problem Outta Control?

Most people would consider a problem out of control when their bird is no longer a welcome, active member of the family, but is an annoying

Take heart: It is possible to live with a content well-behaved parrot.

and frustrating imposition, a danger to itself or others, and a point of aggravation to guests and neighbors. An out of control parrot can make everyone in the household miserable, angry, tense, and sad; these emotions only serve to make the problem worse.

The information in this chapter assumes that you've read the prior chapters and have perhaps come to some conclusions as to why your bird is behaving in a "monster" manner. This chapter deals with how to fix the problems when they have become truly *behavioral*, entrenched in your bird's daily life, and are not just motivated by a current external cause. External causes, such as inadequate housing, poor nutrition, lack of proper attention, and so on, will cause problem behaviors, but these are sometimes easily remedied once the cause is known. For example, a bird that screams excessively may just need a larger cage placed in a more trafficked part of the house. If those changes stop the screaming, that's great; however, they may not, which is when the real work begins.

You have an out of control problem when you are faced with one or more of the following scenarios:

* You feel you have no choice other than to keep the bird locked in its cage all the time.

* You feel you have no choice other than to relegate the bird to a back room, garage, or closet.
* You have begun keeping your bird's cage covered all the time.
* Your landlord is threatening eviction because of your bird's constant noise.
* Your hands, face, and other areas of your body are becoming bruised, scarred, and pulpy from bird bites.
* Your spouse/partner/roommate/child threatens to move out if you don't "do something about that bird."
* You can't go near your bird's cage without it attacking you.
* Your bird loves you to the hostile exclusion of everyone else in the house.
* Your bird has stopped loving you and has become fiercely attached to someone else in the home.
* Your bird is plucking or chewing its feathers.
* Your bird shows signs of repetitive, neurotic behavior, such as beak banging or cage dancing.
* You stay out of your house later and later to avoid contact with your bird.
* Your bird starts repeating you, with phrases such as I hate you and Shut up!
* You dream of releasing your bird back into the wild but can't figure out how to smuggle it to Brazil.
* You've bought this book.

Do you recognize yourself in any of the above scenarios? If so, you're in luck; these situations are rarely permanent. All you need is the ability to deduce why the problem exists and have the time and dedication to take the actions required for solving your bird's problem for good.

First Step: Train Yourself

A problem in any relationship is rarely the fault of just one of the parties involved. In all likelihood, something that a bird's guardian has been doing in the relationship is at fault for creating the behavior problem, or at least for helping it along. Guardian behavior is one of the most common reasons for problem bird behavior. Understanding a little bit about parrot psychology and then interacting properly with your bird will go a long way toward helping to eliminate the problem.

Verbal Reward/Criticism versus Turning Your Back

In a bird's brain there is little difference between verbal criticism and verbal appreciation. Yelling at a

"Are you talking to me?" Reprimanding your bird is not as effective as praise.

bird for screaming is just as effective at rewarding the behavior as is praising it heartily for breaking your eardrums. The trick is to use high-pitched verbal praise and attention when the bird is *doing what you want it to do,* not reprimand it for doing something you don't like. When you yell at a dog or a cat, the animal usually stops what it is doing and retreats. When you yell at a parrot, it's likely to move closer and crane its neck toward you in a posture that looks like it's thinking, "Yes, I'm hearing you, do go on."

Instead of yelling at the bird when it screams, wait for a moment when the bird is quiet and praise it in a soft, high-pitched voice, using its name and a couple of phrases that you use consistently for praise only. Ignoring unwanted behavior and praising desired behavior is the first step to showing your bird what you want it to do and not do. This seems too simple, doesn't it? It works. Your bird will repeat a problem behavior after you jump up and down and cause a scene, but it will not repeat a good behavior unless the praise is just as passionate.

If you remember nothing else, remember this: Drama is the best reward your bird can get for any action, and being ignored is the worst penalty. Turning your back and walking away from a bird that is plucking in your presence or that has just bitten you is far worse for a bird than causing a scene, squirting a stream of water at it, yelling "No!" and so on (remember, physical violence against a bird will never work to solve any problem, and it will only make the problem worse). You only

Find Out What's Working for Your Bird

Just like humans, each individual bird responds to a different way of learning. Some people learn better by seeing something, some by hearing it, and some have to do both. The same goes for parrots. The behavior modification methods you use should be tailored to your parrot's needs. Parrot training literature can only tell you what works for some parrots some of the time; to find out what works for your parrot, you have to experiment with different methods, look for clues in your bird's behavior, and maybe even consult an avian behavior expert. Species matters too; what works for a budgie may not work for a macaw.

have to ignore a bird for a minute or so to be effective, maybe five to ten minutes if you need a break to catch your breath and calm down. In bird-time, five minutes of being ignored may as well be an eternity. Ignoring a bird for hours or putting it in a cage in a quiet room for more than five minutes is cruel and will not effect any change. You have to take a proactive approach to reinforcing good behavior. Allowing a bird to scream its head off in a back room is not a way of ignoring the bird, but of ignoring the problem instead. Your bird needs a hands-on training method to show it what you want.

Take a Meditation Moment

Every time you deal with your "monster" bird, take a moment to close your eyes and count ten deep breaths. This gives you a chance to tone down whatever negative emotion you might be feeling toward the bird or the situation. Parrots are uncannily empathic. They pick up "vibes" very easily and are very sensitive to the nature of those vibes. You can't lie to a bird. If you tense up when your bird plucks a feather in front of you, the bird will know that it has your attention and may view that as a reward. Tension, high energy, and angry, passionate vibes in a household can contribute to a bird's problem. Tone down the energy in the household and make sure you're in a placid state when you interact with your bird.

"Me and my bird" Nikki (the author) and Comet.

I sleep in a room quite far from my birds, with a long hallway, the kitchen, a bathroom, and an air shaft between us. Nevertheless, the *second* I open my eyes my birds start vocalizing. I can wake up at vastly different times, and the birds will be silent until they sense that I'm awake. I can only guess that they are so attuned to me and to the energies in the household that they can feel the difference between when I'm asleep and when I'm awake, even with walls between us.

Excessive Vocalization

One of the most common complaints from a parrot's guardian is that the parrot is too darn loud and/or

The more birds you have, the more noise you'll have to deal with.

persistent in its vocalizations. Not only can a parrot's voice annoy the whole household, but it can cause problems with the neighbors as well. Well, here's some startling news: Parrots are noisy animals and nothing is going to change that. There's no such thing as a quiet parrot unless it's stuffed and on display in a museum. A healthy parrot will vocalize loudly every day, usually just after sunrise and at dusk, though some birds, like parakeets and cockatiels, will vocalize much of the day as well.

Most birds will vocalize loudest at dawn and dusk – this is normal behavior.

The size of the voice is in direct proportion to the size of the parrot. If a parrot is exhibiting normal vocalization patterns and the guardian is *still* annoyed, he/she may have chosen to live with the wrong type of parrot. Cockatoos, macaws, and Amazon parrots are darn loud, and that's just a reality that their guardians are going to have to deal with. A noise problem also has to do with the person who's listening: Loudness is in the ear of the listener. Most people will agree that conures and quakers can be loud and persistent, although others hardly hear them at all. To some, the all-day chattering of budgies is relaxing, while another person is tearing his hair out from the constant noise.

A normal, healthy parrot will kick up a racket at dusk and then go about its day, which includes periods of vocalization and periods of silence, like when it's eating, napping, or playing with toys. Around dusk, the bird will become loud and screechy again, and then settle in to a period of relative quiet until the morning. The loud vocalizations at the beginning and the end of the day can last one to two hours, depending on the individual bird, but one hour is typical. In general, the more birds in the home, the longer the period of vocalization. One lovebird might chatter for an hour; 20 lovebirds will chatter most of the day.

Vocalization only becomes a problem behavior when it falls outside of the natural pattern of dawn/dusk screeching, and starts to happen all day long. Abnormal vocalization is easy to distinguish from normal vocalization; it's repetitive, persistent, and can sound plaintive, terrified, pained, or despondent. Here are a few reasons why you might be hearing more from your bird than usual:

Nanday Conures make sweet, fun companions, though they can be persistently noisy, like most of the conure species.

1. There are other birds around. Birds like to vocalize to one another, and if there's another bird in another part of the house, the two birds are going to be

Giving your bird your undivided attention helps minimize excessive vocalization at that moment.

persistently more vocal than if they were in viewing distance of each other. Perhaps the neighbor just got a new parrot, or there's a bird on the loose outside. Some parrots will even respond to the calls of wild birds. Try a white noise machine or CD to drown out the other birds when you'd like some quiet.

2. The bird is in pain or is scared. A bird that caught its toe in something or is otherwise in pain might scream for its life. A bird that's frightened might screech as well. Perhaps there's something new in the bird's environment that is freaking it out. Every time I wear a new hat, my African grey screams like he's being thrashed with a spiked two-by-four. I have to show him the hat first, let him touch it with his beak, and then I can wear it. Pain or fear can have the opposite effect, however, making the bird quieter than usual.

3. It is springtime and the bird's hormones are surging. More noise during mating season is normal, but a noise problem may be remedied by reducing the amount of light a bird receives in each 24-hour period from 12 or 14 hours down to 9 or 10 hours.

4. The bird is contact calling. A bird that's *contact calling,* screaming or whistling repeatedly to its human family because it can't see them, is not a problem bird. This is a bird whose cage has been ill-placed, or whose owners aren't paying enough attention to it, or who simply wants to know where its owners are when they're out of its sight. Birds are rarely alone in the wild, and they can become fearful and insecure when left alone. The bird continues to call and, if unanswered, will continue to do so loudly and continually until the owner gets fed up and relegates it to the basement or finds it a new home.

The simple solution to shortening the duration of contact calling is to call back, the way the bird's mate would in the wild. My birds call me when I'm out of their sight, and I call back, "Hello, [bird's name] I'm here!" They call me a few more times and I call back again, and then it's over. If I don't call back, they will continue the contact calls for lengthy periods, sometimes 40 minutes or more. I can tell the difference between their normal vocalizations and the contact calls because the contact calls are identical, repetitive, and sound like a question to me.

You can also originate a contact call by using a sound that your bird will respond to from another room, like a whistle, clicking, or a phrase that your bird likes. This is a good interaction to reinforce with your bird in case it gets lost. Think of it like the children's game, Marco Polo—you want your bird to reply every time you initiate the call, the way children yell "Polo!" when the blindfolded child yells "Marco!"

5. The bird screams because there's a rival in its midst. You're playing with your new puppy, talking on

the phone, or embracing your partner. Your bird feels threatened by this behavior (after all, in the bird's mind you should be faithful to it and it alone) and begins screaming to get your attention.

6. The bird learns to scream from its humans' interactions with one another. In some homes, people seek one another out when they want to talk to them; in other homes people yell to one another from room to room. The room-to-room yellers are bound to have a parrot that yells from its vantage point to seek attention from the others. Also, homes where everyone is arguing loudly all the time will tend to create a loud parrot.

7. The bird isn't getting enough attention. This is the foremost reason why parrots scream when they're in a home environment. Most parrots bonded to a human want that human's undivided attention a lot of the time. Cockatoos and cockatiels may want attention all day, every day, and African greys and lovebirds may want attention for a few hours here and there, with breaks in between for snacking and napping on top of the cage. Whatever the case, a bird that's not getting the attention it wants will try to get that attention by screaming (among other behaviors).

Remedies for the Screaming Parrot

Excessive screaming, like other learned behaviors, is a response to unintentional reinforcement. Here's what happens: A bird screams in the middle of the day to get its guardian's attention. This is a new behavior that the bird is programmed to believe will work, but it's not yet reinforced (it doesn't know for sure if the screaming will work). The guardian comes running because something must be wrong. The bird has gotten an initial reward—the guardian's presence. Nothing is wrong, so the guardian goes away again. The bird screams again—and again and again. This time, the guardian is quite unhappy with the behavior and tells the bird "No!" or shouts at it to stop, maybe even throws a shoe at the cage. Wow, the bird thinks, what fun! I've got the power here! Or, perhaps, the guardian is sympathetic to the bird, opens the cage, picks it up and coddles it when it screams, or runs over and gives it a toy or a treat—anything to stop the noise. Again, the behavior is reinforced and will continue. The screaming brings the guardian running, gets the cage open, and then gets attention.

The key is not to reinforce the behavior in the first place, but if it's already entrenched in the parrot's daily routine, there are a few things to try that will help reduce the screaming:

Some Screaming is Normal
Realize that you have to allow the bird certain times and places where loud vocalizing is okay. You should not reprimand or otherwise engage the bird during

Some screaming is normal, and is not cause for alarm or frustration.

Are you paying enough attention to your parrot?

these times—let it vocalize to its little birdy heart's content. Vocalizing is normal and a good way of releasing tension, anxiety, and pent-up energy. Your bird is just being a bird. If normal screaming is bothering your neighbors, create a "screaming room" where your bird can be as loud as it wants. Take your bird there when it's most likely to scream, and stay with it, talking excitedly, singing, and dancing around to give it the idea that screaming and carrying on in that room is okay. This is not a room for punishment, and you shouldn't leave your bird alone in the room. This is a place to have fun and let it all hang out. You can acoustically pad the room the way drummers do so that the noise doesn't bother anyone. The shower also makes a good screaming place; when your bird is most likely to carry on, take him into the shower with you on a suction-cup shower perch and have a duet (don't ever leave a bird in the bathroom alone). Your neighbors can't complain about you singing in the shower, can they?

Pay Some Attention to Your Bird

Maybe your parrot has a right to complain. How much time do you spend with your bird? Is it truly lonely and languishing away, or is it making unreasonable demands for constant attention? Parrots need more than ten minutes of attention before work and a half hour before dinner. Try to include your parrot in your daily routine, such as when you shower, eat meals, and watch television.

Time out: When your bird is screaming for attention and you know that it's healthy, housed well, has had enough food and sleep, and is getting plenty of attention already, it's time for a "time out." You will need to buy another cage and place it in a darkened room away from the activities of the house. Don't put toys into the cage, but do put in some water. Use this cage only for time outs, not for sleeping or traveling.

Choose a distinct phrase and a hand gesture that you will use just before you put your bird in the "time out" cage. For example, when the bird screams, look directly at it with a stern face, say "No scream," and

Parrots need a lot of hands-on love and affection.

then put your fingers in your ears. You can use any phrase and hand movement you'd like, as long as you're consistent. I use "eh-eh" and a finger pointed upwards, as well as a firm gaze. When the bird screams again, take it to the "time out" cage without making eye contact or talking to it; using a perch or dowel rather than your hand is preferable. Be as clinical and as calm as possible. You must only put the bird in a time out after you've used the gesture and phrase and it has screamed again; you have about a five-second window to use the "time out" as a teaching tool—any longer than that and the parrot will not know why it's being whisked away.

Place the bird in the cage and leave the room for five minutes, no longer. If you have to, cover the cage with a dark cloth. When the bird has remained quiet in the cage for a few minutes, remove it from the cage with your hand, talk to it in a low, soothing voice, and take it back to its original spot. The bird will eventually get the idea that when it screams it gets placed in a spot where there's no stimulation. Remember, this "time out" is not punishment, but a learning tool that shows the parrot what you want and don't want. The idea is to get the bird conditioned to stop screaming upon hearing/seeing the phrase/gesture and to stop screaming before you have to give it a "time out."

One problem with "time out" is that the bird might like the "time out" and demand it by screaming, which makes the problem worse. You aren't making eye contact with the bird, but you are picking it up and taking it somewhere—perhaps a place it likes—and this can be very exciting. If "time out" works for you, great; if not, discontinue using it.

Substitution

Often, the best way to get a bird to eliminate one behavior is to substitute it with another, more acceptable behavior. For screaming, show your bird that it can get the same reaction it wants by making a different, pleasant noise, such as

Substitute a quiet noise for a loud one.

whispering, clicking, whistling, or talking. When your parrot is in the middle of its attention-demanding screaming routine, continue doing what you're doing (getting ready to leave the house, cleaning, cooking, and so on), making no eye contact with the bird, but gently clicking, whistling, and whispering to no one in particular. You're not interacting with the screaming bird, but offering it another "language" that you might respond to if the bird mimics it. When the parrot is quiet for a minute, turn your attentions to it and praise it with the same low sounds. When the parrot screams, turn your attentions away from it and start the clicking and whispering again. The bird should eventually start to mimic the low noises that you're making. Great! High praise for that bird! When the bird clicks, whispers, or whistles, pay some attention to it, and eventually the screaming pattern will be broken and replaced by the clicking, whistling, and whispering—we hope. You can even substitute other noises that you won't mind hearing, such as a dog's squeaky toy, but make sure the noise is easy for even the most "untalented" bird to mimic.

Praise for Acceptable Vocalization and the Quiet Bird

If you have a persistently screaming bird that you can "catch" being quiet for even a moment, praise that moment as if the bird just won the Nobel Prize. The same praise should be offered for acceptable vocalizations. The bird will eventually realize that it's getting attention not when it screams, but when it is quiet, talking, whistling, clicking, and so on.

Entertaining the Bored Bird

Some parrots scream because they're bored. Give a screaming bird something to do. Fresh branches from non-toxic, unsprayed trees, toys that require "work," television, and other stimulation should help with excessive vocalization. Keep all of your toilet paper and paper towel rolls, cap one end with tissue paper and a small strip of masking tape, fill the roll with fun things like nuts, sisal rope knots, balled-up paper, dried fruit, and so on, then cap the

Beating Boredom

Parrots easily develop problematic reactions to boredom. It's important to keep a parrot stimulated in the ways that it would be stimulated in the wild—fresh branches to chew, fun food to play with, and a lot of social interaction. Building a natural habitat or a simple safe place for the bird to fly is a great way to allow a bird to be a bird. Flying is a quick way to alleviate boredom, but a captive bird should only be allowed to fly in a place built specifically for flying, not loose inside of the home or out of doors where there are predators.

other end. You can do the same type of thing using white tissue paper that you make into a "gift" for the bird to open. These kinds of interactive toys give a bird something to do other than scream. I give my birds tissue boxes with a few tissues still inside—they love to tear up the box and pull out the tissues.

Chatterboxes

Some people who live with a talking species often wonder where the bird's off button is located. African greys, yellow-naped Amazons, budgies, and other good talkers may spend hours jabbering away to themselves, going though their whole repertoire of words, noises, and phrases. I must admit that it's difficult to concentrate on anything when my grey is shouting, "Come here, come here! I love you. I love you. Whooooo, whoooo, whooooo!"

When Does Your Bird Scream?

Do you recognize a pattern in your bird's screaming that doesn't match the natural pattern of the dawn/dusk vocalization? For example, some birds scream when their guardians get home from work. This often happens because the guardians greet the bird lavishly the minute they get home, and the bird comes to expect it. The bird then screams its head off until they come rushing to its cage. These guardians should ignore their screaming bird and not even look at it for ten minutes after they get home, then they should greet the bird calmly and leisurely. Try to pinpoint when your bird's abnormal vocalization is at its worst. What are you doing at that time that could be causing the ruckus? Have you inadvertently trained the bird to scream?

Talk to Me!

Your parrot won't talk? First, make sure that the bird is a talking species; for example, African greys and Indian ringnecks are more likely to talk than lovebirds. Second, some sexes in some species talk with more frequency than others; for example, the male cockatiel and budgie will be more likely to talk than the female. Is the bird old enough to begin talking? Do you talk to the bird so that it has something to mimic? Some birds, even those in species that can learn to talk, never utter a word. But talking isn't what makes a parrot charming, and it shouldn't be the sole criteria for whether or not a bird is a valuable companion.

Chances are you bought a talking species because you wanted a bird that had the potential to talk. A bird that talks is content and attached enough to its guardians to want to pick up their vocalizations. "Excessive" talking is not like excessive screaming; birds talk and scream for different reasons, though those reasons can overlap. A bird that's talking directly to you is trying to get your attention. A bird that's sitting around jabbering to itself is entertaining itself or is using words in lieu of bird vocalizations.

One theory I tend to believe proposes that a bird will talk when it's displeased or bored at a specific moment (but not in general). For example, Hope, my African grey, will stand quiet and content, eating an apple on the top of his cage, and the second I get on the phone he'll start jabbering loudly. As soon as I hang up he'll stop talking immediately and go back to his apple. He views the phone as a rival and is trying to get my attention away from it. He's disgruntled when I'm on the phone and uses his versions of my own vocalizations to get me to put the rival down and turn my attentions toward him. Instead of trying to discourage him from talking, I just leave the room if I'm on the phone or need a few minutes of peace. Don't discourage your bird from talking once you've taught it to talk; you will confuse it by praising it for talking one moment and then trying to dissuade it from talking the next.

Dirty Words and Come-a-Runnin' Sounds

Curses are probably the easiest words to inadvertently teach your parrot. In general, when someone curses there's a lot of energy and power behind the word, such as when someone stubs a toe or is very angry. These utterances are exciting to a parrot because the words are powerful and may attract attention. The best way to eliminate a curse word is to substitute it for something that sounds like the word, but isn't the word. For example, every time the bird says "damn" you will wait a few seconds and then say "wham" with a lot of emphasis and in your best praise voice. Ignore "damn" and praise "wham," even when it's only you saying it. This is easiest with two people. One person says "wham" and the other praises the person for saying it. The parrot will want to repeat the word that gets the attention, not the one that's being ignored.

Does your parrot have you wrapped around its little claw?

Turn Down the Volume

Parrots that live in loud homes tend to be louder than those that live in quiet homes. Loud television, music, dogs barking, children coming and going, and loud talking or arguing will cause a parrot to want to compete with all of it. What choice does it have? A parrot is designed as an attention-getting machine, and it will adapt its natural resources to get what it wants. Unfortunately, the television is difficult to hear over a loud parrot, so the humans naturally turn up the television, and the parrot has to get even louder to compete. Appliances like the vacuum cleaner, dishwasher, and blender can cause a parrot to scream. Turning down the volume in your home will help to turn down the volume on your parrot.

It's harder to eliminate what I like to call "come-a-runnin' sounds," such as the microwave, a smoke detector that needs batteries, the alarm clock, the door buzzer, and the phone. I call these come-a-runnin' sounds because they are all sounds that alert us to something happening in our environment that requires our immediate attention, sounds that make us come-a-runnin'. These sounds in particular drive me so nuts, I often tell my African grey that if he doesn't stop, I'm going to move out. I've been able to avoid or eliminate all but two: the beeping of a delivery truck backing up and the wailing of fire engines and police cars. I guess that I tense up when I hear these sounds, and though I'm not consciously aware of a change in my demeanor, my grey parrot is.

Ear Plugs?

I'm a writer by trade, and listening to my parrots jabbering, whistling, and squeaking all day doesn't do much for my concentration. In fact, there are sounds they make that feel like someone's running a cheese grater over my brain. Rather than trying to get them to stay quiet all day long while I work, I've invested in an ear-protection headset—the kind that gun enthusiasts use when they're on the rifle range. If I'm really trying to concentrate, I'll put in ear plugs and use the headset. I also tend to work at night now, when the birds are sleeping. Part of being a parrot owner is being willing to change the way you do things in order to live peacefully and happily with your feathered pal.

The reason these noises are so powerful and easily mimicked is because they draw our instantaneous attention. When the phone rings or the door buzzes, we jump up to get it. The same goes for the microwave beeping, the alarm clock ringing, or the smoke detector that's running low on battery power. The parrot puts two and two together and comes up with five: *If I make this noise, the parrot deduces, my human will come immediately to me and pay me some attention.* The logic is faulty, however, because a parrot is not a microwave.

When I go out of town I leave Hope, my African grey, with a friend of mine who has a particularly obnoxious door buzzer. When I come back from vacation, Hope inevitably repeats the sound of the door buzzer over and over—very loudly! When the door buzzes, my friend jumps up to answer it. Hope is no dummy, and he figures that if he makes the same sound, my friend will jump up for him, too. When I get Hope home again, I ignore the sound of the buzzer and it goes away in about three to four days, even when he's been mimicking the sound for two weeks or more. Ignoring sounds that make you nuts and praising sounds that you want repeated should help for the parrot that thinks it's a doorbell.

Biting

Biting is another of the most common complaints from people living with parrots. Most people think that biting is a natural behavioral response, but it's really a learned response that is almost exclusive to birds in captivity. Parrots in the wild do display aggression that *might* lead to biting should an

Biting is a conditioned response, not an instinctual one. This Quaker isn't really biting – he's using his beak for balance.

interloping bird persist in its advances, but it's more likely that one of the two birds involved in a foray will fly away before allowing itself to be bitten. Birds naturally understand each other's body language and can tell when they're going to lose a fight, so they will usually avoid it. Humans can bite one another during a fight too, but it happens far less frequently than other self-defense mechanisms.

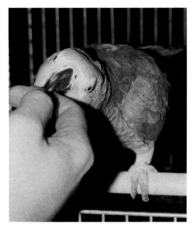

Preventing a bite is easy: learn to avoid it in the first place.

People get bitten when they are unaware of the signals their parrot is sending. The bite is then reinforced by the guardian creating a drama reward for the bird (screaming and moving away from the cage) and the bird learns after one nip that biting is a powerful act. The first key to stopping a biting bird is to avoid the bite in the first place. If there's no bite, then there's nothing to reinforce. Biting birds usually display various signs before they bite, including eye pinning, tail flaring, hissing or spitting, fluffed and defensive posture, and screaming, among others. Do not put your hand near a bird that's displaying these behaviors.

Like screaming, biting is easily taught. Here's a common scenario: Some birds use the beak to test the sturdiness of something it's about to perch on, like a hand, for example. Hope, my African grey, uses his beak for balance, so I offer him both a perching hand and my other hand so that he can grab onto

If you respond with confidence, things will be better for you and your bird.

my finger with his beak and pull himself up. He's a little clumsy, and if I don't offer the other hand for him to grasp with his beak, he's likely to fly off of my perching hand because he may feel that it's not sturdy enough to hold him.

Novices to parrots may not know that a parrot uses its beak for balance, and they will pull their hand away when the bird offers its beak. This quickly teaches the bird to try harder to snatch that finger, and when it does it will latch on more powerfully than it originally would have. The parrot may even make a game of it. Or, the bird will sense that you're afraid and view your hand as something to fear—after all, you become afraid every time the bird reaches for your hand, so there must be something wrong with it, right? The hand isn't safe, and the bird will eventually come to mistrust it so much that it will bite the hand to make it go away. Move slowly and with confidence when handling your bird.

Here are some other common reasons for biting:

Fear
A bird that's scared and backed into a corner is naturally going to bite. It has very few other options and it's programmed to defend itself. Something as

insignificant as a new wristwatch or ring can cause a parrot to become fearful and bite.

Control

If you have been bitten by your bird before it's likely that you retreated from the bite—that's the natural reaction. The bird, however, learns that biting makes you go away, which is what it may want when you're trying to get it off of its playgym to go inside its cage for the night or when it's chewing something it shouldn't. If the bird learns that biting is an effective way to make you leave or perform a "drama dance," it will use biting liberally.

Jealousy

Your bird is fiercely bonded to you. Springtime arrives and your bird's hormones are raging. It views you as its mate, and as its mate, it must defend and protect you. Other people, including your spouse, children, and parents, are considered rivals or threats and will not be tolerated near you. But instead of biting them, your bird bites you. In the wild, a bird will snap at its mate to make the mate fly away to safety. It's not uncommon for a jealous, unclipped parrot to fly into

Beaking

Young birds that are involved in exploring their world sometimes become "beaky," and certain species are more prone to this than others. Beaking is not equivalent to teething in babies, but it's close—just as a human baby wants to put everything in its mouth, so does the beaky baby bird. Beaking is not biting, although some birds can beak hard enough to hurt. Try not to overreact to beaking or you will reinforce the behavior, which can turn into biting. Give a beaky baby a "time out" in its own cage. It may just be excited and need a few moments to itself to calm down the faces of its rivals and bite them, which can be very dangerous. Generally, the person who is bonded to the parrot runs to save the human being attacked by retrieving the parrot. This is a great reward for the parrot, which has now learned that attacking another family member gets the favored family member to come running.

Territoriality

A bird that's hormonal or fearful may become territorial over its cage or another part of the home and will not allow anyone in range of its area without a fight.

Illness

A bird that is ill, injured, sleep-deprived, exercise-deprived, or malnourished is a good candidate for becoming a biter.

Excitement

Some birds can hardly contain their enthusiasm and will bite in response to being overstimulated. Rough or excited play can elicit this kind of bite.

Attention Biting

You're just sitting there peacefully with your parrot, watching television, and then all of sudden, chomp! An attention bite is delivered based upon no stimulus whatsoever. That's the problem—your parrot is telling you that it is present and wants some active attention. My Meyer's parrot, Jesse, was notorious for this kind of biting, so I make sure that I'm actively playing with him when we interact and I've been able to avoid a bite from him for many years.

Remedies for the Biting Parrot

If your bird is already a biter, it is important that you not reinforce any more bites. Your bird will be shocked if you don't react to a bite in the usual way. Have some poise and dignity, and just walk away, the same way you would react to a screaming bird. Jump around, yell, and double over from pain in a place where your parrot can't see or hear you, but whatever you do, don't perform a dramatic "pain dance" in front of it. Biting is easier to quell when you avoid it; work to praise not biting rather than punishing biting, which is not as effective.

The following are some other ways to dissuade a biting parrot:

Stick Training

A biting parrot would do well with some stick training, especially if it's a large parrot with a powerful beak. Stick training is simply teaching your bird to step up on to a stick or perch, as well as onto your hand. This is very important for a bird that's defending its cage (so you can remove the bird easily without being bitten) and one that bites at known times, like when you try to put it back inside the cage. Start by buying a long textured dowel or perch that's the right diameter for your

Stick training is important for any parrot.

bird's feet—it should be able to grip the perch firmly and feel secure being moved around on it. Place the perch near the bird's cage, and move it a few inches closer each day. Finally, put the perch or dowel inside the cage and allow the bird access to it for a couple of days. Once the bird is familiar with the perch, you can begin asking the bird to step up onto it. Most birds that have previously stepped up onto a hand will accommodate. If you know that your bird bites when you remove it from the top if its cage, usethe stick, then have it step off of the stick onto your hand. Do the same for any other "known" biting times. This does not teach the bird not to bite, but it reduces biting and therefore reduces the reinforcement a bird might receive for biting.

The Jiggle Method

A bird that's about to bite will stop in mid-crunch if you jiggle your hand or arm back and forth a little, just enough for your bird to have to stop what it's doing. Once you have the bird's attention, look at it directly and say "no bite" or a phrase of your choice. Now you have an opportunity to put your bird back into its cage or on a playpen without having been bitten and without having reinforced biting behavior. Some people advocate dropping the bird to the floor when it bites; this works to get the bird off of you, but it also can be a drama reward, as well as a way to injure the bird.

Time Out

Use the same "time out" method for biting as for screaming, but make sure that you apply the "time out" immediately after the bite and after looking directly at the bird and saying "No bite" or a phrase of your choice. You have a window of about ten seconds after a bite occurs to turn it into a teaching moment. Remember, remaining calm is key.

Distraction Method

When you know that your bird is going to bite, you can distract it with another stimulus (other than the hand you're offering it to step on) and that will usually stop the bite. For example, my grey parrot never, ever wants to be taken off of the shower perch

Squirting

Squirting a parrot with a stream of water for an undesirable behavior stops the behavior for one moment, but doesn't teach the parrot anything. In fact, it might appreciate the little bath and begin behaving "badly" to get it! Squirting can also freak out a sensitive parrot or reinforce the behavior in a parrot that wants another squirt

after we're done bathing, and he will snap at me when I try to remove him. I look at him with a stern face and very firmly and loudly direct him to get onto my hand. I don't use this tone of voice, which is somewhat like a drill sergeant's, at any other time. I can see by his body language that he knows I mean business, and that the mean face and firm tone distracted him from what he really wanted to do, which was to bite me so that he could stay on the perch. Jingling a couple of pennies inside a soda can or another similar noise will work too, but don't make the noise too scary. This method doesn't really teach the bird not to bite, but it avoids the bite, which is one step closer to living with a non-biting bird.

Keep Handling Your Bird

Many bird guardians get discouraged after being bitten a few times, especially if the bites draw blood, and they begin playing with the bird less and less. Some birds are abandoned altogether; they then become fearful of humans because they have little contact with them. This only serves to make a bird bite more, not less. Gentle, enjoyable, hands-on interaction with humans is the way to discourage a bird not to bite, instilling trust, not fear. Whatever you do, do not use gloves or wrap your hand in a towel to pick up your bird. You will only succeed in terrifying it.

Plucking and Chewing Feathers

Feather destruction is another of the top complaints from people living with parrots. Cockatoos, African greys, eclectus, conures, macaws, and cockatiels are particularly prone to this behavior, though all types of parrots will pluck or destroy their feathers. Plucking, like biting, is a behavior common only to birds in captivity, so humans have to look at what they're doing (or not doing) for a cause. There are two basic reasons why a parrot destroys its feathers: a medical problem and/or the bird is experiencing an environmental, stress-producing disruption.

In all my years living with birds, including various Amazons, macaws, conures, cockatiels, lovebirds, budgies, finches, lories, poicephalus, and my one grey, I've only personally experienced two self-mutilators. Both were lovebirds. One I bought from a pet store

out of mercy because it was obviously older than the others and not feeling well. The little male was indeed ill, and I treated him with antibiotics and an antifungal medication, according to my avian veterinarian's directions. About a year later the bird contracted aspergillosis and I treated him again. He began to pick his chest and belly feathers, even after he became well—aspergillosis is a respiratory infection and the damage done to his system was obviously irritating him. When I kept him in an e-collar his feathers would

Plucking or Disease?

Parrots that self-mutilate only have access to their body feathers; if you notice that your bird's head feathers are also looking shabby and plucked, another parrot might be picking on the bird or there could be a serious medical cause, such as Psitticine Beak and Feather Disease.

These Moluccan Cockatoo feathers have been chewed in half. Chewing is often a response to boredom.

A parrot that is picking in one area may have a medical problem on that site.

grow again, but every time I removed the collar, he picked them out. Eventually, he died an early death. He simply wasn't well to begin with.

The other self-mutilator was my little handfed Fischer's lovebird, Mango. When Mango was five, I moved her to New York City, where I spend part of my year—the other part I spend in Florida. After a few months in New York, Mango began rubbing one side of her face against a perch until it was bald, and sometimes scabbed and raw. I tried everything, but nothing I did helped her for long. Finally, when I went back down to Florida and Mango was back in her big flight cage next to a window overlooking trees and water, she immediately stopped the behavior that she had exhibited for months. Apparently, she didn't appreciate the concrete view from her city window.

One of these instances was medical and one began as a result of an external cause. In my practice as an avian behavior and care consultant, most of the feather destroyers I see have a combination of the two—a high- or low-grade medical/nutritional problem combined with an external change in the bird's life. How the bird is self-mutilating can be a good indication of what's wrong. Here are a few things to look for:

Chewing

Chewing and destroying the feathers may be a precursor to plucking them out; it may also be a response to a low-grade illness or malnutrition, hormone surge, boredom, incessant fear, cage-bound neurosis, change in environment, poor wing clip, or an irritant in the air, such as cigarette smoke.

Does your bird have enough toys? Keeping him entertained often prevents plucking.

Plucking

Plucking the feathers out is more violent than chewing; it can result from many causes, including illness, malnutrition, hormone surge, lack of moisture on the skin, mites, boredom, fear, cage-bound neurosis, poor wing clip, irritants in the air, and a change in environment.

Mutilating

Self-mutilation is one step beyond plucking and involves the breaking of the skin. Causes include all of the above.

That Tastes Bad... But Not That Bad

Applying bad-tasting sprays to a plucking bird's feathers does not work to dissuade plucking and will only serve to make a miserable parrot more miserable.

Site Picking

A parrot that is picking at one particular site generally has an issue with that site, whether it's an infection, injury, or itch. Some parrots have been

Close interaction with your bird helps abate loneliness.

known to mutilate a site, perhaps on the breast or the leg, down to its flesh and bone. Cockatoos in particular are notorious for site picking, and there is no known cause as of this writing.

Becoming a Plucking Detective

Why is your bird plucking? The very first action to take at the onset of your parrot's self-mutilation is a visit to the avian veterinarian. An illness or injury might be plaguing the bird and causing the behavior. Ruling out a medical cause will help you to discover what else could be bothering the bird.

After the veterinarian, take at look at your bird's nutritional status. Does it get enough vitamins and minerals? Fruits, vegetables, cooked and table foods? A bird that's on an all-seed or all-pellet diet is bound to have nutritional problems, regardless of manufacturer claims.

Hormones can play a role in feather picking. A hormone surge may give the bird a rush of energy and a single-mindedness that it didn't have before, and because it may not have an outlet for that energy, the bird may turn upon itself. Easing a bird's springtime hormones by manipulating the light it receives may help stop or prevent it from feather picking. This is a time to bolster a bird's nutrition as well.

A poorly clipped bird may begin to pluck because the ends of its flight feathers weren't cut as neatly as they should have been, and the sharp ends are pricking into the bird's skin. Also, some birds, like the African grey and the Amazon, should not have a severe clip—these birds tend to be heavy, and a hard fall can injure the feathers and cause plucking to begin.

How much time does your bird spend in its cage? How much time do you spend interacting with your bird? A cage-bound bird is a good candidate for plucking, as is one that previously received a lot of attention and is now receiving far less.

How often does your bird bathe? Dirty birds or birds that aren't getting enough moisture on the skin can become itchy and start to bother their feathers.

Beak Banging and Cage Dancing

Repetitive beak banging and cage dancing (when a bird rocks back and forth or nods up and down over and over) are neurotic behaviors indicative of a bird that's "cage bound," pent up too long in a cage that's probably inadequate, with not much to do, and very little human interaction. This is a bird that needs some extra tender loving care, a lot of time out of the cage, and a reevaluation of its living environment. Plucking is probably not far behind for a bird that's exhibiting these neurotic behaviors..

Is there anything new in the bird's immediate environment? Look around the room from your bird's perspective. Is there anything new outside that your bird can see? Is there anything new it can hear? Perhaps a construction crew has started an addition to your neighbor's home, or the city is dynamiting a quarry a few miles away. Birds are very sensitive to changes and may start plucking when they become fearful or annoyed.

Plucking caused by an environmental factor is a bird's response to anxiety that it can't filter though its response system by any other means. It can't fly away from the irritating or frightening environmental cause, nor can it hide. The parrot has little self-direction, which inevitably leads to behavior problems. Once self-mutilation becomes a habit, either because it is self-rewarding (easily distracts from and alleviates stress) or has been inadvertently rewarded by human behavior, plucking is a very difficult pattern to break.

Here's an example you might relate to: When you injure yourself you get a scab or scar tissue, both of which can hurt and itch. It's very tempting to scratch a scab or scar tissue, but you might try not to do it because scratching will make the wound worse. Birds don't have this type of rational reasoning, and they will bite at an irritating or itchy spot, regardless of the consequences. Even when the wound heals, the habit has been formed and will continue. Here's another example: Have you ever bitten your fingernails or had another small self-mutilating habit, such as picking at your cuticles? Why do people bite or pick at themselves? In general, these behaviors begin during a time of stress when there are few other easy outlets. The nails are convenient, and biting them is a good distraction. Eventually, the stressor that started the nail biting goes away (we hope) but the habit remains. It's the same for birds that damage their feathers.

Remedies for the Plucking or Feather-Chewing Parrot

Because each individual parrot self-mutilates for different reasons, I cannot advise a specific program that will work for every parrot. However, once we determine the cause to be environmental, here are some of the successful actions that I advise my clients to take:

Give the Bird Something Else to Do

A bird that is bothering its feathers might need something else to do. Fresh branches with bark and leaves are a great distraction, but make sure they're safe and have not been sprayed with pesticides, fungicides, or fertilizers. Provide additional toys, sisal knots, hard

Your bird's environment can contribute to its stress.

nuts, preening toys, and feathers (you can buy them from craft stores but make sure they're sterile). Invent toys that hide fun objects. Do anything you can to put your bird to work, but make it fun.

Boost the Protein Content of the Bird's Diet

There's a theory that a plucking bird may be getting protein from the ends of its feathers, and instead of discounting this as a cause, I advise upping the protein in your parrot's diet. Include well-cooked egg, tofu and fresh or frozen soybeans and soymilk, chicken and chicken bones, cooked fish, and any other safe protein source your bird will eat.

Give the Bird Some More Attention

Perhaps your bird is languishing away for your attention, and all it has to do to distract itself from the loneliness is plucking. Is the bird getting enough exercise? Playing with the bird more often will help to expend some of its pent-up energy.

Provide More Bathing Opportunities

Misting and bathing a parrot causes it to preen, which provides a distraction from plucking and promotes healthy feather grooming. Bathing also moisturizes the skin; dry skin can be a cause of plucking.

Provide Additional Rest

A bird that's tired all the time is a candidate for plucking. Provide at least 12 hours of dark, quiet rest for a plucking bird.

Use an E-collar

A transparent Elizabethan collar can be placed around a parrot's neck in extreme mutilating situations. This collar will prevent the bird from plucking, but it does not treat the cause.

Stay Calm

As with any other behavior, the humans surrounding the parrot can reinforce the behavior by calling attention to it and even by becoming tense when the behavior occurs. Plucking can become a manipulation game for a parrot, just as can screaming and biting. Ignore plucking and praise for not plucking. Be calm and poised around your bird. Treat it as you would a beloved relative that's recovering from an illness and needs attention, love, kindness, quiet, good nutrition, and some pampering.

Cage Territoriality and Cage Refusal

The bird's cage is its territory, but a bird that's well-bonded to you, trusts you, and wants to share its life with you should be more than happy to share its living space. In the wild, a bird would share its nest with a mate and chicks. Why shouldn't it share its

The cage is a parrot's domain, but you should still have free access to it without being threatened or bitten by the feathered resident.

Building trust – on both sides – will help to eliminate cage territoriality.

space with you, its loving guardian? Parrots will guard their territory from intruders, but your parrot should not view you or other members of its family as intruders.

First and foremost, a bird's cage should be respected as its home, the place where it eats, sleeps, plays, and just hangs out. However, you should have access to it for feeding, cleaning, playing with your bird, and so on, without fear of being bitten. Cage territoriality can be exhibited in all parrots, but it is most dangerous with the larger parrots, which can offer a nasty bite. This behavior is terrible for the parrot, too. A parrot that won't let its guardians near the cage is a parrot that is going to be spending a lot of time alone.

Preventing cage territoriality is as simple as establishing a trusting relationship with a young bird and enforcing and reinforcing two easy commands: step-up and down. You can use any phrase to indicate these commands, but you must always use the verbal command combined with the gesture. For example, when I want my grey parrot to step on to my hand I say "Whoop!" and when I want him to step off, I say "Down." When he wants me to pick him up, he says "Whoop!" It's a nice little communication tool for us. Also, like with other undesirable behaviors, it's important not to reinforce cage territoriality by fleeing

Bring on the Noise

Parrots also need auditory stimulation to remain emotionally healthy. A quiet home is an anxiety-producing home for a parrot. In the wild, there's never a moment of quiet, not even in the wee hours of the night. During the day, the flock is screaming and squawking, making all kinds of noise. When a predator comes into the parrots' range, the first bird to spot it will send up an alarm cry, and all of the other birds will freeze and become quiet immediately (or fly away, whatever seems right to do at the time). This quiet moment indicates that a predator is near and that it's time to be extra observant and cautious. Because your bird is programmed to equate quiet with careful, it will exert a lot of energy vigilantly guarding itself against an invisible predator. Leave the television or the radio on to break the monotony. A CD playing natural jungle sounds or rain is great, too.

the scene, creating drama, or trying to punish the bird.

A bird that is coming into maturity or going though a springtime hormonal phase is likely to become territorial of its space. When the step-up and down commands are reinforced verbally and physically every single day, even a hormonal bird should be conditioned so well that it complies with your requests. However, as a bird matures it seeks more self-direction; it wants more control over its life. Remember, a parrot is an intelligent, sensitive creature, and when it's not hurting anyone, itself, or your property, it should be allowed to live as a self-directed creature (as much as that is possible). But it's important to make sure that the parrot's efforts for self-direction do not cause undesirable behaviors to become reinforced by your behavior.

For example, let's say you approach the cage and your parrot doesn't want to come out and snaps at you. The parrot is trying to assert its will onto the world. Fine. That's normal. But if you then accept that behavior and walk away, the behavior will be reinforced and the parrot will repeat it—this leads to biting and threatening behavior, and you will unlikely be able to come near the cage without a problem. In this case it is important to follow though with your initial action, if only for a moment. There's no reason for you to get bitten in this case, so ask the parrot to step up onto a stick and insist that it comply. Walk a few feet away from the cage and ask the bird to step onto your hand. When it does, praise it again, then put it back in or on its cage and walk away. No drama necessary, and your bird has learned that both of you can have what you want when you want it.

In some cases, the bird's cage may need to be moved to another location until the bird learns that the up and down commands aren't negotiable. Some birds that behave aggressively near the cage will become sweet again when moved to a neutral location where they can't see the cage. But both of these solutions are temporary "quick fixes" and don't solve the problem—only repetitive, positive reinforcement for good behavior will do that.

An older, secondhand, or bronco parrot might be more difficult to work with. After all, you aren't responsible for this bird's behavioral problems, but you are now responsible for eliminating them. In this case, you will have to work with the bird well away from its cage. You don't know what started the behavior, so you have to work on building trust and enforcing your step-up and down commands before you can be sure that the commands will work near the cage. Oftentimes, a secondhand bird is fearful and views its cage as its only safe haven. You don't want to take

If treated properly, your bird will learn that you're not scary.

that safety away from the bird, but you do want the bird to know that you aren't scary but that you will insist on having access to the cage. Again, use high praise for even the smallest good behavior and utter coolness for undesirable behaviors.

Some parrots don't want to go near the cage after playtime—no way, no how—and will refuse in any way it can to go back inside. This bird will bite or will get "weak kneed," as if its legs forgot how to step off of your hand and on to the perch. For the biter, make going back to the cage fun, not just a compulsory "down" command and then the slamming of that iron door. Create a little song and dance as you go back to the cage, something the bird can look forward to and really likes. Don't just rush up to the cage and dump the bird inside. Create a ceremony. The same applies for the "week-kneed" bird.

Why does the bird freak out when you make motions to put it back into its cage? You dump it inside, turn your back, and walk away. You've got other things to do. What a depressing moment for your bird. Spend a few minutes talking to your bird after you put it away, scratching it through the cage bars and offering it treats. Make going back into the cage a positive experience, and make sure the cage is a spacious, entertaining place to be.

One-Person Birds

Does your bird love you, but become enraged, even hostile, when another person is in the room? Perhaps your bird was once sweet to you, but has now bonded with another member of the family and threatens to take your eyes out when you approach the cage.

Two's Company?

Some people at their wit's end with a biting, screaming, hormonal, plucking parrot think, and rationally so, that buying the bird a friend will solve the problem. In some cases that can work, but for the most part, it only makes the problem doubly bad. What if the birds don't get along? What if one kills the other? Unless you have the facilities (and the mental strength!) to live with two parrots you can't control, it's better to try harder to live happily with the one you already have. If you are set on getting another parrot, try searching the parrot rescue agencies first—there are a lot of lonely parrots that might appreciate living with a parrot friend in a good home.

Many species are prone to this behavior: Amazons, macaws, lovebirds, to name just a few. In the wild, many of our companion birds are monogamous and very protective of their mates. When danger comes near, one bird will scream and even snap at the other to make it fly away and avoid the potential threat. Because your bird may view you as its "mate," it may think that it has to protect you—and that kind of protection can sometimes hurt!

Allowing your bird to interact with all members of the family is the beginning to solving "one person bird" behavior.

Before your bird has the chance to exhibit one-person behavior, have someone else in the family take over at least one feeding a day, and ask everyone in the house to talk to the bird, make soothing sounds, and give it special treats. From the very beginning, when you first bring your bird home, make sure that everyone in the home, and even guests, handle the bird so that it learns not to be fearful of family members or new people. In some species possessiveness is unavoidable, but the degree of possessiveness can be lessened by showing the bird that it is part of a family where there are no rivals for attention.

If the bird is already firmly a one-person bird, begin including it in family activities, such as dinner at the table (on its own perch, not the table), where it has to behave like a polite member of the flock. Have other people feed the bird and talk to it. Make sure everyone in the household is gentle and kind toward the bird, which will pick up any vibes of resentment, fear, or mistrust. The cause may be hormonal; you may be able to reverse the hostility by cutting down on the number of hours of light the bird receives per day, as well as bolstering its diet and exercise.

Preventing Problems

The best way to deal with problems is to prevent them. Easy for me to say, right? What if the problem is already happening and is driving you nuts? Well, it's not hard to compound one problem on top of another once a problem has started. This chapter will help you to prevent additional problems, as well show you how to ease the current problems.

How Do You Handle Your Parrot?

Some parrots develop problems because they are being improperly handled by their guardians. Fear can easily develop when a guardian is tentative about

Birds are very sensitive to body language.

handling a bird; birds can sense fear and feel it in our movements. Move your bird around with confidence. A bird should feel secure on your hand or arm—not like your hand is going to drop out from under it.

But I'm Just Being Myself

Birds are very sensitive to body language, and they have natural, genetically programmed reactions to specific human actions that they associate with danger. Here are three typically human actions that may stress out an already stressed bird:

1. Staring

One of the indications of an animal being a predator is that it has eyes on the front of its face, able to stare directly ahead. Parrots, like other prey animals, have eyes on either side of the head so that they can see more of the world around them, enabling them to be more aware of predators in their midst. Humans, a bird's guardians, are predators, and a parrot is naturally programmed to recognize that. A bird that is hand-reared and raised with gentleness learns quickly that humans aren't anything to be feared and will perform copious antics to make its human look toward them. However, a parent-raised or wild-caught bird, or a shy or fearful bird that comes from an abusive home, doesn't know that humans can be friendly, and it will view direct staring—those predatory eyes looking its way—to mean that it is in trouble and perhaps about to be harmed. If you're dealing with a bronco bird, or one that has been hurt by humans in the past, avoid directly staring at the bird until it comes to trust you a little. The combination of staring, approaching, and touching can be too much for a skittish bird, an animal that isn't programmed to understand that a predatory creature isn't always dangerous. For the hand-raised parrot, a firm, direct stare along with a command or gesture can stop an unwanted behavior in its tracks.

Improper Interaction

Roughhousing with a parrot is never a good idea and will only succeed in teaching it to roughhouse back. Rough play may also terrify a bird, an animal that needs love and affection, not a wrestling match. Parrots are very physical creatures in certain ways—they like to have the beak touched, the head and neck gently scratched, and some will allow petting. I knew a macaw that loved a good foot massage. Touch your bird gently and slowly to gain and maintain its trust.

2. Yelling

When two humans argue, it's usually the loudest one who gets heard. It's natural for us to yell louder at someone who's yelling at us. But, our brains can reason, and we can quit the yelling when we feel it's not serving its purpose. A bird doesn't think this way. If you yell at a bird that's screaming, you're reinforcing the behavior—the bird thinks you're playing along, or that you're trying to communicate. The bird will scream louder and with more frequency. Now, when your human brain realizes that yelling at the bird isn't working to shut it up, you stop yelling, but your bird doesn't. Yelling at a bird doesn't get to the root of any problem (even though it can sometimes be satisfying to do so).

3. Shushing

This soothing sound often works well with a human baby, but to a bird it may sound like a snake's hiss, and snakes are one of a parrot's deadliest enemies. Instead of uttering shhhhh, shhhhhh, shhhhhh, speak calmly and in a low, gentle voice. Ticking or clicking with your tongue is also a calming noise for a parrot, which may learn this easy sound and repeat it back to you.

How Birds Learn: Conditioning versus Punishment

Parrots don't understand punishment the way we do. Parrots, like most other animals, live for the moment. They aren't thinking about doing their taxes, whether

it's going to rain tomorrow, or if the Yankees will win the playoffs. They're thinking: Wow, the back of this wooden chair is fun to chew on. Well, maybe they're not thinking exactly that, but you get the point. Instead of punishing a parrot, it's far more effective to teach it what you want it to do using conditioning and praise.

Birds learn more from reward than they do from "punishment."

Have you heard of Pavlov's dog experiment? Simply, Pavlov rang a bell every time he fed a group of dogs. Eventually, the dogs came to associate the ringing of the bell with food, and they would salivate when they heard a bell, even if there was no food present. This is called *classical conditioning,* and isn't really about learning, but creating an association between stimuli. Birds do learn associative responses to stimuli, but they are often unintentionally taught, such as a bird saying "hello" when the telephone rings.

Sometimes you have to become a psychologist to properly understand and modify your parrot's behavior.

Birds learn more effectively though o*perant conditioning,* in which the bird forms an association between a behavior and a result of that behavior. For example, a bird that steps up easily on to your hand has just preformed a behavior that you desire. You reward the bird verbally and perhaps give it a treat. Eventually the bird will realize that when it steps nicely on to your hand, it gets a reward that it likes. When the bird refuses to get onto your hand, there's no reward. Uh-oh.

To take it one step further, if you use a verbal command along with the gesture of placing your hand in the step-up position, your bird will come to associate the verbal command with the reward and will perform the desired behavior (or try to) upon hearing the command. Some parrots will lift a foot upon hearing the step-up command, even if there's no hand present to step up on.

How Much Attention Does a Parrot Need?

Parrots need a lot of attention, probably more than any one human being can give. My clients often want to know how much time, exactly, should they spend with their bird. My best answer is "as much as you can."

There are different levels of attention that you can give your bird, and a combination of these will serve to keep a parrot happy, if everything else in its life is suitable. Think of the attention that you give your bird

Clicker Training

One problem with operant conditioning is that you have to be extremely quick with the reward. For example, you have to praise the bird as it's stepping up on to your hand, because once it's up there for a few seconds, it will have no idea what all the fuss is about, though it will appreciate the attention. Some animal trainers use a "clicker" to indicate to the animal that it has done something right; the trainer clicks the clicker then offers the parrot a treat. Eventually, the parrot comes to associate the click with the treat. Once that happens, it's easy to quickly reward a good behavior because all you have to do is click and the bird will know it has done something right and will wait for its reward. You can use the clicker from across the room too, making it more effective than a food reward, and the clicker can be used by multiple people.

Spend some time just "hanging out" with your bird. Include him in your daily activities.

as a bull's-eye on a dart board. When you're in the bull's-eye you're interacting directly with your bird, holding your bird, making eye contact, and talking to it. In the next ring of the bull's-eye, away from the center, you are hanging out with your bird, but not necessarily interacting directly with it; the bird is eating a meal with you, watching television, taking a shower, and so on. In the third ring away from the center you are in the same room with your bird, but there's no social interaction; your bird can see and hear you, but both of you are doing your own thing. If you can hit all three of these marks every day, you're doing pretty good; but remember, you're aiming at the bull's-eye to win the game.

The Parrot on Your Shoulder
Many bird behaviorists claim that you should never allow your bird to perch on your shoulder. I can't say

Beware of placing an aggressive bird on your shoulder. This peachfront conure looks like he's having fun, and so does his guardian.

"never" to this one. Every bird is different and every relationship is different. It's probably pretty safe to have your cockatiel, budgie, lovebird (well, most of them), conure, or other small bird on your shoulder, although some of these birds may not behave themselves near your face—my Meyer's parrot lost his shoulder privileges long ago.

As for the larger birds, such as cockatoos, Amazons, and macaws, you have to be the judge of your individual bird. Your bird is not trying to dominate you by being on your shoulder. It's trying to be close to the places that give it a lot of stimuli, like your eyes and your mouth. The shoulder is a nice place to watch the world go by. However, these birds are notorious for biting the face and neck in a jealous fit, and that can be very dangerous. You have little control over a parrot that's on your shoulder, so it's not the best perch for an unpredictable bird. I've had Amazons that I wouldn't let near my face, and others that I trusted to sit on my shoulder with not a second of doubt.

Is your bird going to suffer from not being allowed to ride on your shoulder? No, certainly not. My parrots don't use my shoulder for a perch, though I do write with them taking turns standing on the back of my office chair. I suggest giving the bird a chance at your shoulder if you like the pirate look, and if you receive one bite, that's it—no more shoulder. But remember, the large parrots are powerful and can cause the loss of an eye, part of a lip, or ear, so don't say I didn't warn you.

Teaching the Step-Up and Down Commands

Of all the behaviors you can teach your parrot, the step-up command is possibly the most important. This command allows you to retrieve your parrot at any time, and it is especially useful when it's behaving fussy or is in potential danger. Step-up is the act of

The step-up command is important for every family member to learn.

Your bird should readily step on to your finger when you ask
– politely, of course!

your parrot stepping gently on to your hand or finger,
without hesitation, on command. A parrot is not
hatched knowing how to do this, so you must teach
it. Perhaps your parrot came to you already tame and
hand trained—that's great! But it's still important to
reinforce the step-up command so that it becomes
second nature to you and to your parrot.

Assuming that you are teaching a tame or semi-tame
parrot the step-up command, begin by allowing the
parrot to come out of its cage on its own. You win
nothing by fishing the parrot out violently, and you
will only succeed in beginning the session on a bad
note. Place a perch on top of its cage or let the bird
climb on to a standing perch where it will be standing
on a round dowel, not a flat surface. If your parrot is

a youngster you can gently lift it out of the cage, but it doesn't yet know how to step up, so be careful not to pull too hard on its feet.

Once the parrot is out, give it a treat, either a bit of food or a good head scratching. This will show the bird that learning sessions can be fun, and it will look forward to them. Next, begin rubbing your bird's chest and belly very softly and gently with the length of your index finger, talking softly to it, slowly

It's up to you to make learning fun—with a tasty treat, perhaps!

increasing the pressure with which you push on its chest. You may have to repeat this for a few days, depending on the tameness of your parrot. Your semi-tame parrot may not be sure what you are up to, and it might be wary of this attention. Take things slowly and work to gain its trust. A tamer parrot will often sit quietly, enjoying the attention.

Once you feel that your parrot is calm and used to this process, you can increase the pressure you place on its chest. Pushing slightly on a parrot's chest will throw it off balance, and it will lift up a foot to right itself. Place your finger or hand under the foot and lift it. As you do this, tell your bird clearly to "step-up," or use another phrase, as long as you're consistent (I use "whoop"; I like the way it sounds and the parrot can repeat it easily). You must always say your chosen

Learning helps everyone feel good.

phrase when it steps on to your hand; your parrot will come to associate the action of stepping onto your hand with the phrase.

Once your parrot is fairly good at stepping up, you can have it step from finger to finger, repeating the phrase and praising it. Your bird may hesitate at first, but soon it will know exactly what you want. Be sure that your learning sessions last only a few minutes each, and try not to become frustrated if your parrot doesn't do exactly what you want right away. Learning sessions are ideally short, perhaps 10 to 15 minutes a twice a day, and should be incor-porated into playtime.

Most youngsters will learn the step-up command easily, in one or two short sessions, while a semi-tame parrot will take longer. The more your parrot trusts you, the easier it will be to teach it anything. Even if this command is the only "trick" you teach your parrot, is it by far the most valuable.

Once the bird has successfully stepped onto your hand on command a few times, start training the "down" command in the same way, saying "down" (or another phrase) each time your parrot steps down from your hand.

Stick Training

Stick training is simply teaching the "step-up" command using a perch or dowel instead of your finger. It is very important that your parrot know how to step onto a stick. The day may come when your parrot refuses to come down from the curtain rod or gets out of the house and is sitting high in a tree. A parrot that has been stick trained will be easy to retrieve with a long dowel or broomstick. A parrot that is not used to stepping on a stick will be terrified of it and you may lose the opportunity to save your bird from harm.

Stick training is essential – how else will you get your parrot down from the chandelier?

Teach "step-up" with a stick the same way you teach it with your finger. Stick training should begin as soon as you begin hand taming your parrot. If your bird is terrified of the stick, you can leave it close to the cage where your bird will have a chance to view it and get used to its presence. Use different sticks during training so that your parrot learns not to be afraid of various dowels and perches.

Giving Up On the Bird

There may come a time when you feel you have to give up on your bird. Before you do, ask yourself if you've tried absolutely everything you can do to reverse the problematic situation. Have you tried a professional avian behaviorist? Do an internet search and consult someone if you feel you can't do it alone.

If you feel that your bird should be re-homed, please do not sell the bird or give it away to someone who will give it up because of the same problems you're dealing with. Instead, find an avian sanctuary near you and talk with the people who run it about your options. Even though your bird might be driving you crazy or hurting your feelings (and your fingers) it deserves to have a suitable, loving, permanent home.

With the proper care, any parrot can be a friend for life.

Friends for Life

Your companion bird will be around for a very long time, and it is up to you to make the time you have enjoyable and rewarding. Using this book, patience, time and love, you can help your bird not only become part of the household, but a valued family member.

Outta control no more.

Resources

Magazines
Bird Talk Magazine
Birds USA
P.O. Box 6050
Mission Viejo, CA 92690
(949) 855-8822
www.animalnetwork.com

Bird Times
7-L Dundas Circle
Greensboro, NC 27407
(336) 292-4047
www.birdtimes.com

Pet Bird Report
2236 Mariner Square Drive, No. 35
Alameda, CA 94501
(510) 523-5303
www.petbirdreport.com

Books
The Simple Guide to Bird Care & Training
by Julie Rach
TFH Publications, Inc., Neptune City, NJ. 2002

Taming and Training Cockatiels
by Nikki Moustaki
TFH Publications, Inc., Neptune City, NJ. 2002

Parakeets
by Nikki Moustaki
TFH Publications, Inc., Neptune City, NJ. 2002

Birds for Dummies
by Gina Spadafori
John Wiley & Sons, New York. 1999

Guide to a Well-Behaved Parrot, 2nd Ed
by Mattie Sue Athens & Michele Earle-Bridges
Barrons, Hauppauge, New York. 1999

Bird Clubs and Societies

Avicultural Society of America
P.O. Box 5516
Riverside, CA 92517
www.asabirds.org

American Federation of Aviculture
P.O. Box 7312
N. Kansas City, MO 64116
(816) 421-BIRD
www.afa.birds.org

Web Resourceses

Association of Avian Veterinarians
www.aav.org

Avian Yellow Pages.
www.skyeweb.com/ayp/index.htm

Big Bird Search
www.bigbirdsearch.com/search/Companion_Birds/Articles
/Breeding/index7.shtml

Birds n Ways
www.birdsnways.com/birds/articles.htm

Birdy Works.
www.birdyworks.com

Hot Spot for Birds.
www.multiscope.com/hotspot/birdhome.htm

Kaytee Avian Foundation.
www.kaytee.com/avian_foundation/

World Parrot Trust.
www.worldparrottrust.org

Rescue and Adoption Organizations
Avian Rescue Online
www.avianrescue.org/

Bird Placement Program
P.O. Box 347392
Parma, OH, 44134-7392
(330) 772-1627 or (216) 749-3643
www.avi-sci.com/bpp/

Caged Bird Rescue
911 Thomson Road
Pegram, TN 37143
(615) 646-3949

Exotic Bird Rescue Ring
www.neebs.org/birdresc.htm

Feathered Friends Adoption and Rescue Program
East Coast Headquarters
4751 Ecstasy Circle
Cocoa, FL, 32926
(407) 633-4744
West Coast Branch
(941) 764-6048
http://members.aol.com/_ht_a/MAHorton/FFAP.html

For the Love of Parrots Refuge Society
3450 Interprovincial Highway
Abbotsford, British Columbia
Canada
(604) 854-8180 or 8381

Foster Parrots Ltd.
P.O. Box 650
Rockland, MA, 02370
(781) 878-3733
www.fosterparrots.com

The Gabriel Foundation
P.O. Box 11477
Aspen, CO 81612
(877) 923-1009
www.thegabrielfoundation.org

The Oasis Sanctuary
P.O. Box 3104
Scottsdale, AZ 85271
www.the-oasis.org/

NBARC, Inc.
Northcoast Bird Adoption and Rehabilitation Center
P.O. Box 367
Aurora, OH
(330) 425-9269 or (330) 562-6999
www.adoptabird.com

PEAC. Parrot Education and Adoption Center
P.O. Box 34501
San Diego, CA 92163-4501
(619) 232-2409
www.peac.org

TARA. Tucson Avian Rescue and Adoption
(520) 531-9305 or (520) 322-9685
www.found-pets.org/tara.html

The Tropics Exotic Bird Refuge
P.O. Box 686
Kannapolis, NC 28082-0686
(704) 932-8041 or (704) 634-9066
tropics@juno.com

Educational Organizations
The Kaytee Avian Education Center
585 Clay St. - P.O. Box 230
Chilton, WI 53014
(920) 849-2321
(800) 669-9580
www.kaytee.com

Pet Sitters
National Association of Professional Pet Sitters
1200 G St. N.W., Suite 760
Washington, DC 20005
(800) 286-PETS
www.petsitters.org

Pet Sitters International
418 East King Street
King, NC 27021-9163
(336) 983-9222
www.petsit.com

Emergency Resources
National Animal Poison Control Center
(888) 426-4435
www.napcc.aspca.org

Association of Avian Veterinarians
P.O. Box 811720
Boca Raton, FL 33481
www.aav.org

Index

Index

Index

Index

Photos:

Joan Balzarini, Fran Beck, Isabelle Francais, Mike Gilroy, Chris Guido, Bonnie Jay, Alan Kahn, Eric Ilasanko, Horst Mayer, Nikki Moustaki, Robert Pearcy, John Tyson, Louise B. Van der Meid.